W9-BWQ-963

MODERN DRAMATISTS

Modern Dramatists

Series Editors: Bruce and Adele King

Published titles

Reed Anderson, *Federico Garcia Lorca*
Eugene Benson, *J. M. Synge*
Renate Benson, *German Expressionist Drama*
Normand Berlin, *Eugene O'Neill*
Michael Billington, *Alan Ayckbourn*
Roger Boxill, *Tennessee Williams*
John Bull, *New British Political Dramatists*
Dennis Carroll, *David Mamet*
Neil Carson, *Arthur Miller*
Maurice Charney, *Joe Orton*
Ruby Cohn, *New American Dramatists, 1960-1980*
Bernard F. Dukore, *American Dramatists, 1918-1945*
Bernard F. Dukore, *Harold Pinter*
Arthur Ganz, *George Bernard Shaw*
James Gibbs, *Wole Soyinka*
Frances Gray, *John Arden*
Frances Gray, *Noel Coward*
Charles Hayter, *Gilbert and Sullivan*
Julian Hilton, *Georg Büchner*
David Hirst, *Edward Bond*
Helene Keyssar, *Feminist Theatre*
Bettina L. Knapp, *French Theatre 1918-1939*
Charles Lyons, *Samuel Beckett*
Gerry McCarthy, *Edward Albee*
Jan McDonald, *The New Drama 1900-1914*
Susan Bassnett-McGuire, *Luigi Pirandello*
Margery Morgan, *August Strindberg*
Leonard C Pronko, *Eugene Labiche and Georges Feydeau*
Jeanette L Savona, *Jean Genet*
Claude Schumacher, *Alfred Jarry and Guillaume Apollinaire*
Laurence Senelick, *Anton Chekhov*
Theodore Shank, *American Alternative Theatre*
James Simmons, *Sean O'Casey*
Ronald Speirs, *Bertolt Brecht*
David Thomas, *Henrik Ibsen*
Dennis Walder, *Athol Fugard*
Thomas Whitaker, *Tom Stoppard*
Nick Worrall, *Nikolai Gogol and Ivan Turgenev*
Katharine Worth, *Oscar Wilde*

Further titles in preparation

AMERICAN ALTERNATIVE THEATRE

Theodore Shank

Professor of Dramatic Art
University of California, Davis

89-688

St. Martin's Press   New York

First published in the United States of America in 1988

Printed in Hong Kong

ISBN 0–312–02126–7

Library of Congress Cataloging-in-Publication Data
Shank, Theodore.
    American alternative theatre/Theodore Shank.
        p.   cm. — (Modern dramatists)
    Bibliography: p.
    Includes index.
    ISBN 0–312–02126–7 (pbk.): $14.95 (est.)
    1. Experimental theater—United States.   I. Title.   II. Title:
American alternative theater.   III. Series.
PN2266.5.S5 1988
792'.022—dc19

Contents

Editors' Preface

Modern Dramatists is an international series of introductions to major and significant nineteenth and twentieth century dramatists, movements and new forms of drama in Europe, Great Britain, America and new nations such as Nigeria and Trinidad. Besides new studies of great and influential dramatists of the past, the series includes volumes on contemporary authors, recent trends in the theatre and on many dramatists, such as writers of farce, who have created theatre 'classics' while being neglected by literary criticism. The volumes in the series devoted to individual dramatists include a biography, a survey of the plays, and detailed analysis of the most significant plays, along with discussion, where relevant, of the political, social, historical and theatrical context. The authors of the volumes, who are involved with theatre as playwrights, directors, actors, teachers and critics, are concerned with the plays as theatre and discuss such matters as performance, character interpretation and staging, along with themes and contexts.

Modern Dramatists are written for people interested in modern theatre who prefer concise, intelligent studies of drama and dramatists, without jargon and an excess of footnotes.

BRUCE KING
ADELE KING

Photographs not credited are by
Theodore Shank

viii

Acknowledgements

In particular I want to acknowledge the extraordinary help Adele Edling Shank has given me on this book. She has assisted with her insights and criticism, she has edited my writing, and she has put aside her own work to take charge of the numerous details of preparing the book for publication. Furthermore, her own playwriting has enriched my understanding of the possibilities of theatre.

The directors and other artists who created the works discussed have been generous with their conversations, interviews, and correspondence.

I am grateful to the editors of journals who have published my articles on alternative theatre and thus have provided opportunities for me to develop and organize my ideas on the subject. In particular I thank Michael Kirby of *The Drama Review* for inviting me to serve as a Contributing Editor and Bonnie Marranca and Gautam Dasgupta of the *Performing Arts Journal*.

Several photographers have been generous in allowing me to use their photographs. Especially, I thank Gianfranco Mantegna for his photographs of the Living Theatre. I regret that in a few instances the photographers are anonymous and I have been unable to give proper credit for their work.

Finally, I am grateful to Ruby Cohn for her continuing encouragement over the years.

Foreword

This book is concerned with an on-going theatrical movement in which individual artists or companies create their works autonomously from inception to performance. The works exist only in the audible, visual, and social circumstances of performance. If a script exists, it has either been devised after the performance or served as a step along the way; it is not an end in itself. In some instances a text is not extractable from the production. The text, if there is one, can only vaguely suggest the finished work, and as a result few are published.

A book dealing with such work must take a different form from one concerned with plays that are predominantly verbal and available to the reader through publication. Because the productions are more perceptual than verbal, only the work of artists and companies I have seen can be included. Because it cannot be assumed that the reader has seen the productions, as much attention has been given to descriptions and photographs as space permits. I have chosen for discussion only work I respect and which is also exemplary of the major tendencies of the alternative theatre in America.

The book draws heavily upon my personal experience of these works in performance, upon my notes and photographs, and upon my conversations, recorded interviews, and correspondence with those who created them. My own experience as a director and participant in such works has, I believe, given me additional insight.

New American Dramatists, the book in this series by Ruby Cohn, parallels my book in that it focuses upon playwrights whose work is predominantly verbal and is available through published scripts.

1
The Alternative Theatre

The social upheaval in the United States during the 1960s and early 1970s
not only gave rise to a new cultural movement outside the dominant culture;
it also spawned an alternative theatre. Initially, the new theatre was expressive of those who aligned themselves with the various social movements of
the time – civil rights, free speech, hippie, anti-nuclear, anti-Vietnam War,
ecology, feminist, and gay. It was an alternative to the theatre of the dominant complacent middle-class society which tended to perpetuate the *status
quo* in its aesthetics, politics, working methods, and techniques. The alternative theatre companies directed themselves to the new audiences, often a
specific constituency such as intellectuals, artists, political radicals, workers,
blacks, Chicanos, women, or gays. They explored new working methods,
new techniques, and new aesthetic principles that would be in harmony with
their convictions and could be used to express their new theatrical conceptions.

By the mid-sixties there were five kinds of theatre organizations in the
United States other than the new alternative theatres. (1) There were
theatres which existed as part of the training programmes of colleges and
universities. These were increasing rapidly and were distinctly American,
as only later did a few such programmes develop in Europe. (2) There
were amateur theatres which served primarily the recreational needs of the
participants whose occupations were outside the theatre. (3) The commercial professional theatre of Broadway presented productions intended as
business ventures and, if successful, they were packaged and toured to
major cities around the country. (4) The participants in Off-Broadway
theatres were seriously pursuing theatre professions even though they often

1

received only token salaries for their theatre work and subsidized themselves and their theatres by working at non-theatrical paying jobs. In the late forties and early fifties such theatres were formed not only in New York, but in Dallas, Houston, Washington D.C., and San Francisco. At the outset these theatres were the vanguard of the time, presenting productions from the new absurdists such as Genet, Ionesco, and Beckett, as well as new American plays and plays from the classical repertoire which, because of their limited appeal, were not of interest to the Broadway theatres. By the mid-sixties, however, because of increased production costs, some of these theatres began to choose productions which would rival Broadway. (5) Beginning in 1963 with the founding of the Guthrie Theatre in Minneapolis, large regional repertory theatres were formed in major cities throughout the United States to produce plays from the classical repertoire and Broadway. At first these theatres were subsidized by municipalities and private foundations, then in 1965 with the establishment of the National Endowment for the Arts they began to receive federal subsidy. It was the first U.S. government support for theatre since 1939 when funds for the Federal Theatre Project were discontinued.

When an alternative culture and life-style began to take shape in the mid-1960s, another kind of producing organization came into being. In part it was a grassroots movement in that some of the participants did not come from the theatrical profession but were drawn to theatre as a means of expression for their social and political commitment. On the other hand, in the early sixties New York theatre professionals had begun to form off-Off-Broadway theatres such as Cafe Cino and the La Mama Experimental Theatre Club. These became the new vanguard, taking up the slack left by the increasing conservatism of Off-Broadway. These two strands – the grassroots and professional theatrical experimentation – were intertwined and produced the unique qualities of alternative theatre.

At the outset, it was the new life-style which made these theatres an economic possibility. Within the alternative culture it was not only acceptable to drop out of the established culture's universities and employment, but it was also desirable to withdraw the support of one's labour and tuition fees. It became both a necessity and a badge to live frugally – used clothing, inexpensive shared housing, food from money provided by middle-class parents, food stamps, unemployment benefits, welfare. As time passed, many of the theatres began receiving subsidies from private foundations and from municipal, state, and federal governments.

For the individual participant, the theatre companies frequently served as a total community. Often out of necessity, the companies provided theatre training because the participants had none and because the objectives, techniques, and styles of the new work required skills which were not taught in the universities nor practised in the older theatres. The theatre group and the work in which they were engaged provided the individual with family, work, education, and recreation. It also provided a social experience not usually available in the established culture as membership in these companies cut across traditional lines. Working side by side on an equal basis were students, teachers, theatre professionals, amateurs, people of different races and social backgrounds, those with artistic commitment, and political activists.

The two energizing forces of the new theatre – the moral energy of social causes and the spirit of artistic exploration – gave rise to two perspectives from which artists viewed human experience. There were those who looked outward, exploring human beings in society, analyzing social institutions, considering political issues, and sometimes advocating social change. The other perspective was inward-looking and involved a consideration of how we perceive, feel, think, the structure of thought, the nature of consciousness, the self in relation to art. In the late sixties and early seventies those groups with a social perspective were predominant; but after the successes of the civil rights movement and the withdrawal of American military forces from Vietnam, companies and individuals focusing on intuition, perception, and form were in the ascendancy. Some theatres disbanded, others remain active after fifteen or twenty years, and new ones continue to be formed.

Regardless of perspective, these groups have many things in common which set them apart from the established theatre. Unlike the commercial theatres, they are not primarily concerned with entertainment as a product to be sold. Instead, they are anxious to improve the quality of life for themselves and their audiences. The theatre of the absurd had reflected the philosophical alienation of the individual; the alternative theatre tends to reflect the commitment of the group. The traditional theatrical spaces are economically unfeasible and artistically unsuitable. They are too large and typically are divided into stage and auditorium which dictates a particular performer–spectator relationship unacceptable to many artists on aesthetic grounds and to others because the arrangement hinders the development of a community spirit. However, the most important changes are the development of an autonomous creative method, a shift from the dominance of words to a visual emphasis, and an aesthetic that keeps spectators conscious of the real world rather than focusing them exclusively on a fictional illusion.

An autonomous method of creation became the typical means of making new plays. Instead of the two-process method of the conventional theatre – a playwright writing a script in isolation and other artists staging it – the autonomous method involves a single process wherein the same artists develop the work from initial conception to finished performance. In part the development of this method was a reaction against the psychic fragmentation the artists experienced in the technocratic society which believed that human needs could be satisfied by technical means requiring a high degree of specialization. Instead of the individual specialists of the established theatre, the typical member of an alternative theatre has broad creative responsibilities.

3

Despite the automonous method of creation, the structures of alternative theatre companies vary greatly. Some early groups did not distinguish between the work of performer, director, designer, and playwright. Some collective theatres embraced the idea that everyone should do everything regardless of skill. But as idealism faded and artistic commitment came to overshadow social commitment, the collective method became less rigidly democratic. After its reformation as a collective the San Francisco Mime Troupe did not publicly identify the responsibilities of individual members, but specific directors and playwrights were selected from the company for their productions. Joseph Chaikin was the director of the Open Theatre in New York throughout its ten years, but the productions were created by the entire group under his guidance. In other instances playwright–directors such as Richard Foreman and Alan Finneran have the primary responsibility for the creation of a work from inception to performance.

A visual focus became an alternative to the established theatre's dependence on words as the chief medium of expression. There was a distrust of words because of the end to which they were used by politicians and advertising. It was also recognized that some experiential concepts cannot be expressed by words, and it was thought that society, having relied upon words, had tended to cut itself off from its experience. Furthermore, the alternative culture denigrated nationalism which in part is perpetuated by national languages. Painters and sculptors who were beginning to create theatre productions were naturally inclined toward visual means, and other theatre artists experimented with non-verbal sounds, with placing focus upon the performer's body, and with a variety of other non-verbal means.

With few exceptions, alternative theatre performances are intended to be perceived as existing in real time and place. If one were to devise a continuum of audience consciousness in relation to performance, it would extend, on the one hand, from the spectator's complete awareness of perceiving to, on the other hand, complete psychic absorption into the fictional world created by the performance. Since the nineteenth century when the auditorium lights were turned off during performance so as to focus attention exclusively on the fictional stage events, theatre artists have attempted to make spectators forget where and who they are. This objective continued with even greater success in talking motion pictures. It is the intention of these productions to cause the audience to focus on the fictional illusion being presented and to become psychically absorbed in it to the extent that they lose their self awareness – to make them perceive characters, not the actual performers; to focus on the evolving fictional action, not the tasks of actors as they create the illusion; to concentrate on the fictional time and place of the play and lose their consciousness of the real time and place in which the performance is being presented. By contrast, most artists of the alternative theatre adopted a spectator–performance relationship similar to that in the visual arts. Spectators in a gallery do not lose consciousness of themselves or of the time and place of the exhibition. While viewing a painting they remain aware that the illusion presented is in fact an illusion and they are also conscious of the means used to create it. Similarly, in the work of most alternative theatres the audience is aware of both the illusion and the performers.

Some theatre artists were drawn to the new aesthetic in their attempts to discover the unique possibilities of live theatre as distinct from motion pictures and television. The most important condition of theatre that distinguishes it from these newer media is that performers and spectators are physically present in the same time and place. This is abrogated, however, when the spectators are permitted only to see the illusion of character and not the performer, when they are focused exclusively on a fictional time and place. If a compelling all-absorbing realistic illusion were to continue as the aesthetic means of live theatre, then live theatre would be doomed to compete unsuccessfully with motion pictures.

Among alternative theatre workers there was general suspicion of the illusionistic theatre because of its apparent use of pretence and the mystique surrounding it. There was much talk about demystifying the theatre. Those who advocated the use of theatre to help bring about social change saw a similarity between the function in society of religion and of the all-absorbing illusionistic theatre. Both distracted their constituents from the real world and helped them mentally escape from social problems. For these social activists it was essential that the audience be made to focus on the real world where the changes were needed. Furthermore, it was important to create a sense of community among the spectators who then would have the potential for collective action. Such a community was possible only if the spectators were psychically present.

Models for a focus on the actual could be found in performance situations outside the theatre. The success of a cabaret performance does not depend on audience belief in a fictional illusion. The spectator's focus during circus performances is on the events happening in real time and place. A story teller is viewed as himself in the present even if telling of past events or demonstrating how a fictional person moved or talked. And athletic events consist of tasks performed by individuals without resorting to illusion.

An influx of visual artists into the theatre was a major impetus toward theatre of real time and place. Painters and sculptors, who in the late 1950s were discontent with their traditional static media, began creating happenings in which they hoped to eliminate the separation of art and life. As in theatre these works used environments, performers were engaged in tasks, and there was a controlled time dimension; however, as in painting and sculpture, the spectator perceived them in real, rather than fictional, time and place. Even though the spectators were physically within the environments and sometimes even participated in the events, they were not psychically involved with a fictional world.

In practice this focus on the actual takes many forms and theatre artists have invented or rediscovered numerous techniques. Jerzy Grotowski of the

5

Polish Laboratory Theatre influenced American theatre artists by his actor training method which put into focus actual responses of the body by eliminating all impediments between impulse and reaction. Through his psycho-physical exercises he hoped to eliminate the disparity between the actor's physical and psychic functions. Joseph Chaikin, director of the Open Theatre, also sought to focus attention on the actor's body and voice. His non-illusionistic actor training exercises were designed to intensify what he called the 'presence' of the *actor* as distinct from the *character*. Such exercises became part of the performance in some Living Theatre productions, and in *Paradise Now* (1968) spectators participated in some of the exercises. Members of the company, including Julian Beck and Judith Malina, performed various tasks as themselves. Even when performers represented characters, there was a dual focus on the characters and the performers.

Most guerrilla theatre events of the late sixties and early seventies consisted of tasks performed without a time and place illusion whether or not characters were represented. Abby Hoffman threw real money on the floor of the New York Stock Exchange and the real stock brokers scrambled for it. At a demonstration in Washington in 1970 a black man exhibited himself tied to a cross. Others symbolized the carnage in the Vietnam war by smearing themselves with blood from a slaughterhouse and carrying animal entrails.

The style of acting developed by the San Francisco Mime Troupe permits actors to create an illusion while keeping the audience aware of the real world. We acknowledge the presence of the performers who seem to be demonstrating the characters rather than pretending to be them. Furthermore, the group uses non-illusionistic popular entertainment techniques – juggling, dancing, a band playing familiar music – as the means of attracting spectators in a public park and these techniques are sometimes incorporated into the productions.

In some environmental theatre performances the audience moves from place to place which helps them perceive the events in the present. The same perception occurs in some of Richard Schechner's productions when several focuses are offered simultaneously. The spectators, free to shift attention from one event to another as they wish, structure their own time; the events are viewed as happening in real time much as when watching a three-ring circus. When Snake Theater incorporates into a performance the actual environment of the beach and ocean, the spectator is simultaneously aware of both the actual and the fictional.

The new formalists, coming to the theatre from the visual arts, brought with them an interest in composition and other formal elements, and their productions put these into focus rather than emphasizing a compelling illusion. Some of the resulting works, such as those by Alan Finneran, are animated compositions of objects, projections, and the tasks of performers. Other productions, as in the case of Robert Wilson, have a hypnotic effect somewhat like music, and some make one conscious of structure as in the work of Michael Kirby's Structuralist Workshop.

Those artists who used themselves as the content of their work focused on actuality in another way. Richard Foreman's plays reflect directly his natural thinking processes. The work of Spalding Gray and Elizabeth LeCompte of the Wooster Group presents events from Gray's life using both documentation and imagination. The space in which Squat Theatre performs is separated from the sidewalk by a storefront window so that the actual passersby become part of the performance for the audience inside and vice versa.

Because in the alternative theatre there is no need to keep the audience focused on a fictional illusion, a linear cause-and-effect plot creating suspense is not of pre-eminent importance. This has been the traditional technique for keeping the spectators focused on the evolving future of the fictional characters, on what is about to happen, rather than upon the actual present. It is a psychic state in which one does not perceive keenly and is somewhat like the way one experiences the non-perceptual art of literature. When reading suspenseful fiction one is unaware of the words on the page and focuses only on the fictional events happening mentally. In the new theatre aesthetic it is not desirable to empty the spectator's mind of perceptual values, which are often of primary importance.

The artists who comprise the alternative theatre explore the relationship of the artist to the work and the performance to the spectator. They attempt to discover the unique possibilities of live theatre, and seek ways of extending the use of theatre beyond its entertainment and financial functions. They set out to find or invent more expressive ways to articulate what they know about being alive in the changing times, about society, about perceiving, feeling, and knowing. Of necessity they find new materials, develop new techniques, and create new forms to hold and express this knowledge because the theatrical conventions cannot express the concepts they consider important.

The conventional theatre is usually expressive of a time past. Artists convey through their works a knowledge of how it feels to be alive in their particular time and place. Those concepts, materials, and techniques which are particularly expressive are imitated by others and become conventions. As time passes and these conventions persist, they may cease to convey insights about life in the new circumstances. The realistic box set, for example, may have been particularly expressive in the late nineteenth century when the new social sciences were suggesting that humans, like other biological organisms, should be studied in their environment. But its continued use in the mid-twentieth century became a mere convention. Similarly, the concepts and techniques of the theatre of the absurd expressed the absurdity of life in the 1950s at a time of social and political complacency while governments were adding to their stockpiles of nuclear weapons. While some artists perpetuate such conventions, those who are identified with the new alternative theatre look afresh at the artist's primary source: human experience – emotive, perceptual, intellectual, and social.

2
Primary Explorations

In the early 1960s there were two alternative theatre groups which, because of their commitment, their experimentation with creative processes, and their development of new techniques, had a profound impact upon many who followed. Both companies developed methods of collective creation, but they had distinctly different basic objectives – the Living Theatre, while engaging in aesthetic exploration, came to use theatre as a means of bringing about social change; while some members of the Open Theatre were politically committed, they devoted their work solely to aesthetic experimentation.

When Julian Beck and Judith Malina formed the Living Theatre in 1951 their radicalism was only aesthetic. Since then they have explored a variety of theatrical techniques, some adapted from happenings and aleatory music, they have experimented with group living, and since about 1964 they have committed their lives and their work to an anarchist–pacifist political view with unwavering tenacity. The life-style of the company and their production techniques became models for other new groups in America and Europe, but none has had the commitment, the skill, the persistence, or the longevity, of the Living Theatre which continues to work under its original directors.

The Open Theatre was founded by Joseph Chaikin and directed by him throughout its existence (1963–73). Although Chaikin had been a member of the Living Theatre, his new company avoided overt political content in its productions. The actor training exercises developed by the group, as well as their improvisational techniques for collective creation and their performance style, have been used by many other alternative theatre companies.

The Living Theatre

'Life, revolution, and theatre are three words for the same thing: an unconditional NO to the present society.' This view was expressed in 1968 by Julian Beck who, with his wife Judith Malina, founded and continues to direct the Living Theatre. For three decades they have committed themselves to theatrical and social experimentation which has more than once led to imprisonment.

Beck and Malina met in New York as teenagers and were married in 1948. In 1951 they formed the Living Theatre. For the first few months their productions were presented in their apartment. When Beck inherited six thousand dollars they rented the Cherry Lane Theatre but eight months later it was closed by the Fire Department. From 1954 until 1956 they performed in a loft at Broadway and 100th Street but that was closed by the Building Department because 65 seats were considered too many for safety. More than three years passed before they again had a place to perform. In January 1959 they opened a 162-seat theatre in a former department store at Sixth Avenue and 14th Street. In October 1963 they were evicted by the Internal Revenue Service for non-payment of nearly 29,000 dollars in federal excise and payroll taxes and their last New York theatre closed.

During these first twelve years Beck and Malina were formulating their view of theatre. Beck says that they wanted a revolution in the theatre similar to those which had already taken place in painting and sculpture. They were reacting against naturalism and were primarily interested in experimenting with poetic language. They began by producing the non-realistic plays of people they knew such as Paul Goodman and plays by Gertrude Stein, Brecht, Lorca, Rexroth, T.S. Eliot, Jarry, Auden, Cocteau, and Pirandello. While they worked together in close collaboration – he as designer and director, she as director and performer – their plays were not developed collectively. Their theatre work and their political convictions were at first separate.

Beck had become a dedicated anarchist–pacifist before the first production of the Living Theatre. He had dropped out of university and taken as his mentors Thoreau and Gandhi. Both Beck and Malina were arrested at sit-ins and demonstrations. This defiant, individualistic behaviour was reflected in their theatre works which were intended to jolt the audience into a new awareness, to present entirely unique works, and to explore production techniques which would alter the usual audience–performance relationship.

The search for uniqueness involved experiments with putting actuality on stage which led eventually to eliminating the separation between art and life, between dramatic action and social action, between living and acting, between spectator and performer, and between revolution and theatre. The first blurring of the line between fiction and reality was in Paul Goodman's *Faustina* (1952), named after the wife of Emperor Marcus Aurelius. At the end of the play the scenery disappears as Roman civilization crumbles and

9

the performer of Faustina comes forward. She chastises the audience for not leaping on stage to stop the murder which has taken place. The power of the moment came from a shift of audience perception from the illusion of Faustina to apparent direct communication by a performer. Of course the implied criticism of the audience had no real basis. The stage events were clearly illusory. The spectators were no more guilty in watching them than the performers in enacting them. However, it was the beginning of direct audience confrontation by the Living Theatre, a technique used extensively in later productions.

Similar perceptual shifts were achieved in works making use of the play-within-the-play technique which created an ambivalence in the spectator's mind between fiction and reality. The first of these was Pirandello's *Tonight We Improvise* (1955). After a three year hiatus Beck and Malina opened the 14th Street theatre with *Many Loves* by William Carlos Williams. As the audience enters the theatre, electricians and actors on stage are attempting to replace a blown fuse. When the lights are restored the play begins.

The most important of the productions using the play-within-the-play technique was Jack Gelber's *The Connection,* which Beck and Malina read in the summer of 1958. They were also reading *The Theatre and Its Double* by Antonin Artaud, whose concept of the 'theatre of cruelty' articulated their own feelings about the theatre. Like Artaud, Beck and Malina wanted not merely to entertain but to affect the audience so deeply that it had a cleansing effect. Beck wrote that the problem was 'how to create that spectacle . . . that would so shake people up, so move them, so cause feeling to be felt . . . that the steel world of law and order which civilization had forged to protect itself from barbarism would melt'. This was necessary because that 'world of law and order . . . cut us off from real feeling'.[1]

The Living Theatre felt that *The Connection* was successful in arousing such feelings. They claimed that during its run fifty men fainted. When the spectators enter several heroin addicts are waiting on stage. Another man steps off the stage and explains that he is the producer. He introduces Jaybird as the author and explains that he has induced several real addicts to come to the theatre and improvise on Jaybird's themes for a documentary film which is being shot by the two camera men who are in attendance. The addicts have co-operated in return for a promised fix. They are waiting for Cowboy to arrive with the heroin. During intermission the addicts pan-handle the audience, and in the second act Cowboy arrives and rewards each with a fix.

The dramatic device was that of a play within the play, but the unsuspecting spectators took it for authentic real-life events. The play is not structured conventionally in terms of story, suspense, dramatic pace. The characters simply wait for Cowboy to arrive, put on a Charlie Parker record, play improvized jazz, and get their fixes. Except for the violent reaction of one junkie who overdoses, it seems to be the tempo of real life.

At first Beck and Malina were pleased with this production, believing they had achieved their objective of putting reality on stage and eliciting from the audience a true emotional reaction rather than the modulated feelings orchestrated by traditional drama. In fact it was one of the three productions they took on their first European tour in 1961. However, they were eventually disturbed by what they came to think of as their dishonesty in deluding the audience. They wanted to put reality on the stage, not pretence.

Their next attempt took a new tack. Under the influence of John Cage, who was exploring the use of chance in musical composition, they produced in June 1960 *The Marrying Maiden,* by the pacifist and libertarian poet Jackson MacLow. The text consisted of words or groups of words chosen by a chance system from the *I Ching* and various acting instructions – five different vocal volumes, five tempos, and a hundred or more adverbs and adverbial phrases such as 'gayly' or 'sorrowfully'. Their placement had also been by chance and they determined the feeling with which the actor was to read the text. In performance other chance elements were introduced and the 'acting' of the performers was transformed into actual tasks. The Dice Thrower rolled dice. Every time a seven came up a card was drawn from a pack of cards on which actions had been written. The card was presented to the actor whose turn it was to speak and the action was incorporated. When a five was thrown a sound tape of the actors reading the play, prepared by John Cage, was turned on. Another five and the tape was turned off. Every performance was different.

The frequency of new productions was decreasing – a sign of growing financial difficulties. Longer runs meant decreased production expenses and the directors were spending increasing amounts of time on financial matters. In the last three years before the 14th Street theatre was closed Beck and Malina produced only four plays. Two of these were by Brecht, including *Man Is Man* in which Joseph Chaikin, the future founder and director of the Open Theatre, played Gayly Gay. Thematically the play expressed the directors' growing anarchistic concerns about the loss of individual identity. Of greater importance to the development of the Living Theatre aesthetic and its non-violent convictions was *The Brig* by Kenneth Brown, which opened in May 1963 and was their last production in New York.

Kenneth Brown had been a prisoner in a U.S. Marine Corps brig in Japan. His play is a detailed documentary of routine life in such a prison. The prisoners' activity is totally controlled by the prison system codified in the regulations of the brig. A white line is painted on the floor across each doorway. Even when carrying out an order a prisoner is required to ask permission to cross the line – to enter the toilet, the compound, the storeroom. Speaking to other prisoners is strictly forbidden. No movement or speaking without orders from the guards is allowed. The oppressiveness is intensified by the frequent repetition of the sentence 'Sir, prisoner Number – requests permission to cross the white line, sir'. Any mistaken movement or phraseology is punished with a punch in the stomach, pushups, or other strenuous exercise which pushes the prisoner to the edge of

1. *The Brig*, **photo: Gianfranco Mantegna**

endurance. There is no conventional plot, only the structure of routine – jump out of bed, stand at attention, go to the toilet when ordered, do regimented exercise, carry out precise cleaning assignments, and when no other orders are given stand at attention reading the Marine Corps manual. It is the epitome of an anarchist's hell. It is an environment made suffocating by restrictions which, they hoped, would make the audience gasp for freedom. Director Malina and Beck felt that the production should make the audience want to break down all prison walls. Prison had become for them a metaphor for what Malina called 'the Immovable Structure', whether that structure is 'a prison or a school or a factory or a family or a government or The World As It Is'.[2] Of course, it was not only a metaphor for a repressive society, but the actual means of punishing those who failed to observe its restrictions.

The production brought together several strands of Malina's and Beck's aesthetic and social ideas. First, the production advanced their attempts to present reality. The play was a documentary account of Kenneth Brown's experience rather than a fictional story. The set reproduced the brig in which Brown had been imprisoned. And the performers actually underwent the punishments prescribed, which sometimes resulted in minor injuries, so there was no separation between what the actors experienced and what the spectators observed. Many of the infractions and penalties were improvised in rehearsals, where the usual informality and personal interaction were replaced by a set of rehearsal regulations which paralleled those of the brig,

and there were prescribed penalties for infractions. In performance, however, these actions were absorbed into the stage illusion of a prison, and the
actors represented prisoners and guards. Beck saw that their work differed
from Artaud's theatre of cruelty in that Artaud imagined horror could be
created from the fantastic. To Beck horror is not in what we imagine but in
what is real. He hoped that the production would cause the audience pain,
that it would 'produce real horror and release real feeling'.[3] Second, the
production helped formulate his and Malina's ideas of the prisoner as victim.
In Beck's view *The Brig* exposed the authoritarian nature of American
society and the barricades which divide people into victims and execution-
ers; it put into focus the concept of imprisonment and violence as physical
and psychological repression. Third, when the Internal Revenue Service
closed the theatre in October 1963, it further strengthened his and Malina's
view of the 'money system' as a destructive force. Beck came to 'realize that
the entire economy is strangling most of the creative efforts', and this led to
his conviction that 'the work you do in the theatre' must attempt 'to do away
with the whole system'.[4] The Living Theatre from the beginning had experimented with radical aesthetic concepts and had held radical political views.
Now they were convinced that their theatre should serve a political purpose.
Their lives, politics, and art were coming together.

When the I.R.S. told the company to leave the theatre on 14th Street, the
actors and directors refused. Borrowing from the methods of passive resist-
ance used to accomplish racial integration, they sat in. A further act of civil
disobedience took place two days later when they gave a final performance
of *The Brig* in the padlocked theatre. They were joined in this act by forty
spectators who climbed over an adjoining roof and into a window. After the
performance they were again told to leave, and when they again refused
twenty-five people were arrested. The following summer the Living Theatre
began its voluntary exile in Europe. Beck and Malina returned only briefly
in December 1964 to serve their prison sentences of sixty and thirty days
respectively.

From September 1964 until August 1968 the Living Theatre performed
exclusively in Europe. Leading a nomadic existence they moved through
twelve countries, usually giving only one or two performances in a place.
Twenty-eight people set out from New York. Some left, others joined and at
one time there were over forty in the company. They lived communally and
frugally and they made their most innovative works.

The first piece made in Europe, *Mysteries and Smaller Pieces,* embodied
most of the innovations typifying their European productions. *Mysteries*
consisted of nine segments made up of exercises and improvisations
described as 'a public enactment of ritual games'. There was no text, no set,
the performers wore their own clothes and did not play defined characters.
For the first time there was an opportunity for spectators to participate
physically and in one segment some of the performers sometimes performed
in the nude. Although in one segment there was the suggestion of a fictional

13

plague, the production as a whole did not present a fictional world as the context for the action. The production did not attempt to project a place other than the actual theatre or performance space nor a time other than the actual time of the performance.

At the beginning a man stands at attention on stage facing the audience for about six minutes. At first the audience expects something to happen. When it doesn't they are provoked and become hostile, yelling jokes and insults. Another part of the audience puts down the first. Actors run up and down the aisle while others chant the words from a U.S. dollar bill. A woman sits on stage improvising a Hindu raga in Sanskrit which seems to go on and on. Part of the audience continues to be hostile, thinking the performers are making fun of them by making them listen to noise rather than entertaining them. After a time the rest of the company moves through the audience carrying sticks of incense which they give to the spectators. Julian Beck sits on stage intoning slogans of peace and freedom. The actors return to the stage, sometimes a few spectators follow, and a swaying circle is formed. A performer begins to hum a tone and one by one the others join in harmonizing for perhaps fifteen minutes. This exercise, called 'The Chord', had been introduced by Joseph Chaikin in his work with the Open Theatre. The final segment of Part One involves performers, seated at the front of the stage, doing a yoga breathing exercise.

Part Two is in three sections. Four vertical compartments stand side by side facing the audience like closets without doors. In the darkness four performers enter these boxes and freeze in improvised tableaux. The lights flash up for a few seconds, then go out as other performers take their places in the compartments or in front of them. Each team of four performers creates ten to twenty tableaux. In some performances a few performers are nude. Another exercise from the Open Theatre follows. Actors form two lines facing each other. One performer improvises a sound and movement which is adopted by another performer who changes it and passes it on to another. The final segment is inspired by Artaud's 'The Theatre and the Plague', in which he describes the effects of a devastating plague on the body and mind and draws an analogy to theatre. This is the only segment in which the actors create a fictional illusion. The performers enact the physical and mental deterioration caused by the plague as they crawl and writhe toward the audience. In approximately thirty minutes the wailing ends; they are all dead, scattered in the aisles. Several actors collect the rigid corpses one by one and pile them like logs. In some performances spectators participated. Some died with the actors and were placed in the pile, some tried to comfort the dying, others touched the bodies, hit them, or tickled them to get a response.

On several occasions fights broke out among the spectators who were anti- or pro-*Mysteries*. Other performances were stopped or banned by the authorities because of the nudity of some performers or the participation of the spectators who refused to be controlled by officials. The power of

2. *Mysteries and Smaller Pieces*, **photo: Gianfranco Mantegna**

Mysteries was discovered almost by accident. The first performance was put together on short notice to provide an evening's entertainment in exchange for rehearsal space provided by the American Center for Students and Artists in Paris. The company used whatever came to mind – exercises they had recently learned from a visiting member of the Open Theatre, yoga exercises which some of the performers had been doing on their own, an idea that occurred to Beck when he saw some boxes backstage, etc. The company had not previously considered using these in performance. However, the audience reaction was strong and *Mysteries,* with variations, was performed a total of 265 times – more than any other Living Theatre production.[5] It contained most of the innovations for which the Living Theatre became known during their years in Europe – audience confrontation, spectator participation, breaking down the separation between stage and auditorium, collective creation, performance improvisation, performance without text, set, or costumes, nudity, focus on real time and place rather than a fictional illusion, and actors devoid of the usual stage mannerisms, voice, and bearing. These innovations were intended to unite the actors and spectators into one community in the here and now; their objective was to effect social change. The performers were surprised by the antagonism they frequently created, but they also created zealous devotees.

Frankenstein, the second European production, opened in October 1965, but underwent major changes. The original idea had come from Mary Shelley's novel *Frankenstein, or the Modern Prometheus* but was also influenced by the Jewish concept of the Golem and by films including Chaplin's *Modern Times*. It had been developed collectively by the company as a whole through research, improvisation, and discussion, then was shaped and put into focus by Beck and Malina. The setting imagistically was an elaboration of the tableaux segment of *Mysteries*. It consisted of fifteen cell-like compartments of metal scaffolding in a three-storey arrangement six metres high. The performance took place in these compartments and on the stage floor in front of them.

The performance is non-linear and sometimes the action is indecipherable. It begins with the opening technique used in *Mysteries*. Fifteen performers wearing their own clothes sit on stage facing the audience. They do not speak or move, but approximately every five minutes an amplified voice explains that the performers are meditating in order to levitate the woman seated in the centre. After twenty minutes or so it becomes clear that the levitation has failed. (The Living Theatre is reported to believe that if the concentration is sufficiently intense the woman will levitate and the performance will end.) However, disbelieving spectators become annoyed at being forced to await the impossible. Rather than blame themselves for the levitation failure, the group on stage blames the woman and puts her in a coffin. An actor objects and is hanged. Someone says 'No' to the hanging and is executed. One by one individuals object and are executed in the compartments. They are beheaded, crucified, shot, electrocuted, or guillotined until only Frankenstein and two others are left. As Frankenstein works with a corpse centre stage, the compartments in the structure come alive as a representation of the world. Frankenstein asks, 'How can we end human suffering?' An old woman takes body parts from a bag and fits them to the corpse, then recites an incantation written by Beck.

> Human suffering need not be
> When you master three times three
> . . .
> These body organs from the grave
> Are all you need to make a slave.

Eventually the Creature is represented in three different scales. There is a human-sized version played by an actor, there is one as high as the three-tiered structure with a performer representing each arm and leg, and finally a profile head the full height of the structure is formed by plastic tubing with lights inside.

Much of the language is collaged passages from Mao, Walt Whitman, Marx, Bertrand Russell and Shakespeare, and current newspaper items. When the Creature first speaks near the end of Act Two, it is one of the few straightforward speeches in the entire production. In a passage from Mary Shelley's novel the Creature tells of his discovery of the physical world – darkness, light, fire, etcetera – and his discovery of society – division of

3. *Frankenstein*, **photo: Gianfranco Mantegna**

property, wealth, poverty – and his rejection by it. The rejection generates hatred and revenge which cause new acts of violence. The Creature disappears and Frankenstein and his assistants look for him in the auditorium. In Act Three the actors in the auditorium are captured, interrogated, fingerprinted, and imprisoned in the cell-like compartments of the structure. The prisoners revolt and kill the guards, Frankenstein starts a fire in his cell and the screams of dying prisoners are heard. The structure of society is the cause of perpetual violence. The only positive note is at the very end when the Creature, again created in giant proportions by the bodies of actors, raises his arms in a gesture of peace.

The two-and-a-half-hour performance is intended as a metaphor for the evil in each human being, the monster in each, which comes together to form our societies which perpetuate violence. The compartmentalized physical structure animated by performers is a visual articulation of the structure of

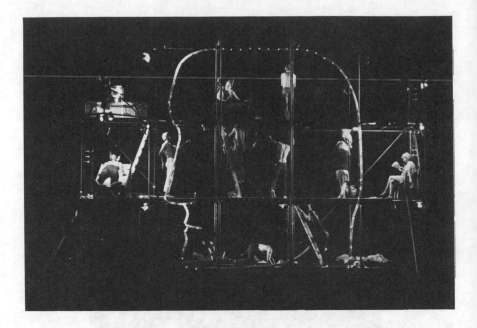

4. *Frankenstein*, **photo: Gianfranco Mantegna**

society. This concept led to a rehearsal technique in which individual performers contributed an autobiographical element by confessing crimes they had committed. According to Malina and Beck it was 'an ugly and painful rehearsal technique' which infected their daily lives. But the search for the 'evil madness' in themselves was essential for 'this evil that is corrupting all the great efforts of man is in each heart'.[6]

Except for Beck as Frankenstein each actor devised, chose, and played several roles. In some instances these roles were abstract. In one section they played qualities of mind such as Love, Imagination, Intuition, Ego. At times the performers created non-verbal vocal sounds for an environment such as the sound of wind and waves aboard ship, and they also mimed these elements through descriptive movement. As in *Mysteries* performers improvised during parts of the performance.

The production was more coherent than *Mysteries,* was more compelling visually, and presented more explicitly than ever before the Living Theatre's view of the relationship of the individual and society; but it was a theatrical metaphor. Except for the opening meditation scene, the entire performance was in the form of a theatrical illusion. Even those task-derived elements were absorbed into the fiction. So, while the production developed new theatrical techniques, it was a retreat from the development of a new means of presenting reality, from theatre as life itself.

Their next production (February 1967) was Judith Malina's translation of Brecht's version of Sophocles' *Antigone*. It again embodied the company's anarchistic views, but its text was more akin to the earlier New York work. It was natural that they would be drawn to a play contrasting the pacifism of Antigone with the tyrannical government of Kreon and demonstrating the civil disobedience of Antigone as a necessity of conscience.

As in *Mysteries* and *Frankenstein* the opening of the performance creates hostility in the audience. However, this time it is used to a different end. The auditorium represents Argos, the stage is Thebes. The Thebans are at war with the Argives for their iron mines. When the performance begins, actors enter and begin staring at the Argive audience; they look it over, they talk among themselves about what they see. When the apparent coldness of the performers toward the spectators is repaid in growing hostility, the war begins. The sounds of gun shots, air-raid sirens, aeroplanes, bombs, troops marching are all created by the performers as they enter the auditorium to attack the enemy. Polyneices, who in the Brecht version is a deserter from the Theban army, having refused to participate in an unjust war, is sur-rounded and killed among the spectators. For many the play seems to be a metaphor for the war which the United States was waging against Vietnam. The spectators are the victims. Julian Beck hoped that 'if people feel how atrocious it is to kill each other, if they feel it physically then perhaps they'll be able to put an end to it'.[7]

The script of *Antigone* was Malina's precise translation of Brecht's text with only a few minor deletions, but the company's acting techniques were continuing to develop. The performers again wore their everyday clothes, there were no sets or light changes, props were mimed, and all sounds were created by the voices and bodies of the actors. The elders of Thebes are Kreon's throne. Four performers become the prison walls enclosing Antigone, and when Ismene belatedly asks to share with Antigone the responsibility for burying Polyneices, the walls cover their ears. Beck says they wanted to eliminate the 'handicrafts of civilization' and put the focus on 'the physical presence of the human being'. This was aided by keeping the twenty or more actors in view throughout the performance. From the begin-ning the Living Theatre had wanted to 'destroy the conventions of theatre', but Beck had come to see that all of their early experiments 'had been bound inside the theatre of the intellect' and were products of 'rational civilization'. Beginning with *Mysteries* they had been attempting to find a basis for acting other than everyday behaviour. This led in *Antigone* to expressionistic movement and vocalization requiring each actor to unite what is said with 'an actual physical locality in the body'.[8] The monstrosity of the system which Antigone must face is represented by a writhing compact mass of actors in which the individual seems to have given up his freedom to the control of the whole.

While in *Antigone* the Living Theatre had retreated from collective crea-tion of the text, they had further developed the concept of the presence of the actor – that is, causing the spectator to focus more on the live actor in their presence than upon the fictional character enacted. It was a tendency

5. *Antigone*, **photo: Gianfranco Mantegna**

already being explored by Jerzy Grotowski of the Polish Laboratory Theatre and it was becoming the main focus of Chaikin's work with the Open Theatre. All three companies were attempting to eliminate the rational control of body and voice which restricted the actor to what could be conceived in advance. They wanted to discover a mode of acting which would be more authentic, more present, because there would be no conscious barrier or impediment between the impulse and the physical or vocal response.

By putting the physical presence of the actor in focus, even in a work using a fictional illusion of time and place, the Living Theatre had taken another step toward the presentation of reality. In their next production, *Paradise Now* which opened in July 1968, they used this concept in a production which in its entirety was created collectively by the company and then, as with *Frankenstein,* structured and edited to its final form by Beck and Malina. Although the production received only 84 performances – fewer than *Mysteries* (265), *Frankenstein* (89), and *Antigone* (172 excluding its revival in 1980) – it is the production for which they became notorious because it involved audience participation to a greater extent than any other Living Theatre work and caused the greatest difficulties with the police and other authorities.

Frankenstein and *Antigone* had been preoccupied with the repressive nature of contemporary culture; the company wanted the next production to be optimistic. In the published introduction *Paradise Now* is described as a spiritual and political voyage for the actors and the spectators. Its purpose 'is to lead to a state of being in which non-violent revolutionary action is possible'.[9] In the anarchist society envisaged the individual would no longer be a slave of money, of sexual taboos, of repressions by the state respecting freedom of movement and other restrictions. The result would be a non-violent society 'in which we simply produce freely what is needed . . . and then use the rest of the energy and the rest of the time of our lives for other things'. Beck and Malina believed this economic social revolution could happen only if simultaneously there was 'an interior revolution, a spiritual change'.[10] With *Paradise Now* they hoped to aid this interior revolution by changing the perception of the audience, by making them realize that a transformation is possible and urgent.

The play is in eight sections, eight rungs of a ladder depicting 'a vertical ascent toward permanent revolution'. This is graphically shown in a chart distributed to each spectator. Each rung consists of three parts: a ritual ceremony performed primarily by the actors, a vision consisting of an intellectual image also primarily by the actors, and an action introduced by the actors and performed by the spectators with the help of the actors.

In the first rung, 'The Revolution of Cultures', the performers present 'The Rite of Guerilla Theatre'. They move in the aisles from spectator to spectator speaking and then shouting repeatedly various statements: 'I am not allowed to travel without a passport.' 'I don't know how to stop the wars.' 'You can't live if you don't have money.' 'I'm not allowed to smoke marijuana.' 'I'm not allowed to take my clothes off.' To demonstrate this last prohibition they take off as much of their clothing as the law permits. The Living Theatre believes that society makes one ashamed of one's body, which causes a disunity between the physical and spiritual self, but if a harmony between these two selves could be achieved, all destructive urges would be eradicated.

The 'rite' of the first section is followed by 'The Vision of the Death and Resurrection of the American Indian' in which the performers sit cross-legged on the stage passing a peace pipe, then form five totem poles, and finally mime being shot by the white man. The 'Action' which follows is initiated by the performers encouraging the spectators to 'Act. Speak. Do whatever you want. Free theatre. Feel free. You, the public, can choose your role and act it out.'

The first section was intended to open people to new values and to discard the old values represented by specific prohibitions of the culture. Section Two, 'The Revolution of Revelation', was intended to describe the aims of the anarchist revolution. It begins with actors gently touching spectators and speaking softly to them. During the Vision part of this section the actors form with their bodies the words ANARCHISM and PARADISE.

Rung Three is 'The Revolution of Gathered Forces'. According to the play the people are now ready to work together for the revolution. During the Action part of this rung discussions are begun on the formation of revolutionary cells for radical action to continue work during and/or after the performance.

6. *Paradise Now*, **photo: Gianfranco Mantegna**

Rung Four, 'The Exorcism of Violence and the Sexual Revolution', is concerned with sexual repression, 'the fundamental taboo that is channeled into violence'. It begins with 'The Rite of Universal Intercourse' in which the performers lie on the stage floor in their semi-nude state entwined in a mass embrace – caressing and undulating. Spectators who join in are welcomed. Those who wish to temporarily pair off and sit face to face with sexual organs in contact, but because of legal restrictions they do not make love. In the Vision which follows actors in pairs are executioner and victim. The executioner mimes shooting the victim who falls and rises to be shot again. The action is performed twenty times. After a time the victim begins to speak gentle words to the executioner who answers with the prohibitions stated at the beginning of the play. Finally they embrace and the scene ends. In the Action portion of Rung Four the spectators are led back into 'The Rite of Universal Intercourse' in which 'the actors/guides seek to consummate the action by a sexual unification'. As a consequence 'the division between actor

7. *Paradise Now*, **photo: Gianfranco Mantegna**

and public diminishes'. Hostilities can be eradicated in the act of physical love. The actors proclaim, 'Fuck means peace'.

Rung Five, 'The Revolution of Action', concerns the individual in relation to the anarchist community, the disappearance of conflicts between Jew and Christian, Black and White, Young and Old, I and Thou, once the money system and its coercive bribery are abandoned. It is a view of the future as are the following sections. Rung Six, 'The Revolution of Transformation', is the period of struggle between the non-violent revolutionary forces of love and wisdom and the reactionary forces of violence. 'The Revolution of Being', Rung Seven, gives glimpses of the post-revolutionary world. In the Action portion the performers and voluntary spectators participate in a trust exercise which became popular with other theatre groups. One person, standing on an elevated place, flies with arms outstretched into the arms of others waiting below.

The eighth and last rung, 'The Permanent Revolution', ends with the company leading the audience into the street as they say, 'The theatre is in the street. The street belongs to the people. Free the theatre. Free the street. Begin.' The ending is not to be mistaken for the revolution, it is an enactment or a demonstration. Nevertheless, it was their intention to bring the spectators to a state where non-violent revolutionary action was possible. An interior change was a necessary prerequisite to the external social and economic revolution.

8. *Paradise Now*, **photo: Gianfranco Mantegna**

For the Living Theatre life, revolution and theatre had become one. The Action portion of each section of *Paradise Now* consisted in part of unrehearsed actual behaviour of performers and spectators without a fictional illusion. The company generally avoided going beyond legal restrictions during a performance as they had no wish to spend time in prison. It was not unusual, however, for spectators to smoke marijuana, burn money, or take off all of their clothes.

Malina and Beck were much influenced by the May 1968 uprising of students and workers in Paris which occurred while *Paradise Now* was being prepared for its short run at the Avignon Festival that July. At the end of the second performance about two hundred people surrounded the Living Theatre in the street celebrating their sense of new-found freedom. It was too threatening for the mayor of Avignon and the company was asked to

24

substitute another work for *Paradise Now*. Instead, the company withdrew from the Festival.

Some French students had criticized the Living Theatre for working within the bourgeois system, accepting contractual arrangements from established organizations and performing in theatres subsidized by the state. When they took *Mysteries, Antigone, Frankenstein,* and *Paradise Now* to the United States for a seven-month tour in 1968 there were other criticisms from the political left. While their rejection of authority, their non-violence, their sexual freedom, and marijuana smoking gave them a rapport with the hippies, their anarchist revolution was not the revolution envisaged by young Marxists and other political radicals who felt the Living Theatre was out of touch with the American situation and naive in believing radical change could be brought about by non-violent means. Indeed, major changes had taken place during their four-year absence. Students had been radicalized through demonstrations against university authoritarianism. They were subjected to arrest and police violence. Only a month before the arrival of the Living Theatre hippies were being transformed into radical Yippies at the Democratic Party convention in Chicago where demonstrations were met with police brutality. The non-violent stance of blacks had been eroded by the Watts riots in Los Angeles, the F.B.I. persecution of the Black Panthers, and the assassinations of black-power advocate Malcolm X and civil rights leader Martin Luther King. A split within the Students for a Democratic Society led to the creation of the Weathermen, an underground organization dedicated to the destruction of property as a means of disrupting the establishment.

The Living Theatre was caught between the reactionary forces of the establishment and the criticism of political radicals. Following the first U.S. performance of *Paradise Now* when they led the audience into the street, they were arrested and charged with indecent exposure, breach of the peace, and interfering with an arresting officer. Performances were cancelled more than once and the Internal Revenue Service impounded their receipts and bank accounts. On the other hand radical spokesmen criticized them for being a part of the institutional framework of the established society and the revolutionary movement considered them irrelevant. Surely the performance of *Paradise Now* in Berkely must have seemed artificial. The confrontation of spectators with such lines as 'I am not allowed to smoke marijuana' seemed frivolous compared to the student-police confrontations in the streets. During this U.S. tour Malina and Beck became aware for the first time of the American revolutionary movement, and it was instrumental in their dicision to stop performing plays *for* middle-class audiences in theatres and begin performing in the streets *with* people whom they considered the slaves of the privileged.

Their American tour had attracted large audiences, much larger than had come to their own theatres in New York. They had become accepted at least as a novelty, but they came to doubt their effectiveness. Some spectators might participate in *Mysteries* and *Paradise Now,* even follow the company into the street at the end of a performance, but the performance was perhaps no more than a memorable evening's recreation. The lives of their middle-class audience and society remained unchanged by the experience. Malina and Beck came to believe that they were being assimilated as other trappings of social change were assimilated, thus forestalling a fundamental change in the structure. Even the words 'revolutionary' and 'radical' came to be used in the programmes of President Nixon and in advertising new products.

Back in Europe in early 1970 the Living Theatre announced to the news media that it was dividing into four cells which would have different orienta-tions. However, only the one directed by Malina and Beck endured. The announcement stated the new objectives. They did not 'want to perform for the privileged elite anymore because all privilege is violence to the under-privileged'. Therefore, they did not 'want to perform in theatre buildings anymore'. And they did not 'want to be an institution anymore' because 'all institutions are rigid and support the Establishment'. It was necessary, furthermore, to liberate themselves 'as much as possible from dependence on the established economic system' and to 'survive through cunning and daring'. Finally, it was essential to find new art forms which would serve the needs of the people.[11] The idea of giving free performances outdoors and thereby minimizing dependence upon the economic system was not new in the alternative theatre movement; the San Francisco Mime Troupe had been giving free performances in the parks since 1962. But when Beck and Malina led their group to Brazil where they performed with and for the poor worker families, they became the first missionaries. However, unlike mis-sionaries of a colonial power serving to contain the indigenous population, the Living Theatre functioned more as a guerrilla band hoping to spread the revolution. And in the end they were treated like other enemies of the state.

From spring 1970 until their arrest in July 1971 the company lived in several communities of Brazil, developing and performing plays which were to be part of a projected cycle of 150 called *The Legacy of Cain,* a reference to the origin of violence. These plays, mostly using movement, sound, and gesture, without dialogue so as to escape problems of censorship, were presented for poor workers and their families in public squares, factories, and the slums where they lived. It was important to make these plays in con-sultation, sometimes with the collective participation of the residents so as to avoid an attitude of superiority. Furthermore, it was the intention of the group to deal with the life and aspirations of the community in which the work was presented.[12]

Judith Malina had come to the conclusion after the American tour that her theatrical life had been spent working for the oppressors. Even *Paradise Now,* she said, was an attempt to shake up this audience. It became clear to her, however, that it was not these people who would make the revolution; it would be made by the economically and culturally deprived. She was deter-mined to put herself 'at the service of the revolution'. In Brazil they discovered that the circumstances of life tend to make the deprived workers accept their situation rather than attempt to change it. In the words of Julian Beck they accept 'a sado-masochistic view of the world' as the natural order. 'The Brazilian woman is a servant to her servant husband' who 'goes to work and gives his body over to the boss.' On an international scale the worker is a slave of the middle-class in the so-called developed countries for whom he produces coffee and sugar at near starvation wages. The Living Theatre hoped to raise the 'revolutionary consciousness' of these people so that when the right time came they would be organized and prepared to 'seize the power' and 'take over the means of production'. As a 'revolutionary artist' Beck wanted to help 'transform the world from a master–slave economy and psychology into a structure or system which is no longer parasitic and exploitive but rather creative'.

Little progress was made toward these goals during the thirteen months the Living Theatre worked in Brazil. They experimented, however, with techniques for involving the people in collective creation. At first to make money, they worked in São Paulo with a group of university students whom they charged for lessons. Together they made a play which was performed only twice in the public squares of a nearby truck-farming village and a proletarian mill town.

In December 1970 they performed a new play in a slum community of about 800 on the edge of São Paulo. They made four visits to the community in advance, tape recording answers to such questions as 'What are your dreams, what do you want to do, how is your life here, what is the community like?' These were edited and collaged and used in a section of the play.

The play begins with a procession of twelve actors singing 'What is life? What is love? What is Death? What is money? What is property?' etcetera.[13] They place a box containing the props in an open area and take positions around it in six pairs representing the bases of enslavement – Money, Love, Property, The State, War, and Death. A Storyteller tells a simple story about each as the corresponding pair of actors mimes the action which ends in a master–slave position. For the next section a loudspeaker is placed on the box and taped voices of the inhabitants are heard. A repetitive song follows.

> My life is 1 hour for 50 *centavos* [about 4p]
> My life is 2 hours for 1 *cruzeiros* [about 8p]
> My life is 4 hours for 2 *cruzeiros*
> My life is 8 hours for 4 *cruzeiros*
> . . .
> My life is 40 years for 87,600 *cruzeiros*

Each master and slave sign a contract with their red thumb prints. Each master binds his slave with a rope, chain, or strap, and then the masters bind each other until only Death remains. The Storyteller tells about the future which ends with a question: 'How did the people free everyone so that the Treasure Box could be opened so that everyone could eat the Celebration Cake and be merry?' The spectators untie the actors, the Treasure Box is opened revealing a large cake which is eaten by the actors and spectators as they talk.

The company came to realize that to avoid working superficially with the people it would be necessary to stay in one place for an extended period. So they went to Ouro Preto, an aluminium mining town of 40,000, with the intention of staying about eight months. At first they taught physical exercises and yoga in the schools. One of the schools asked them to help make a Mothers' Day play and they seized the opportunity. They asked the eighty children ranging in age from seven to fourteen to write down a story or dream about their mothers. The stories were sifted and codified according to content and then dramatized in terms of the same six aspects of the world which had been used earlier except that they substituted 'Time' for 'Death'. The children, attached to their mothers with crepe-paper umbilical cords, were led on a journey through The House of Money, The House of Love, and houses representing the other worldly causes of bondage. Then Big Mama (one actor on the shoulders of another) played a game with the children, whipping them with a crepe-paper whip as they danced and spun until dizzy while those parts of the children's stories dealing with punishment were being read: 'My mother punishes me because she is always right.' 'When she hits me it is because I am bad.' At the end of the performance the children broke their umbilical cords by jumping from a platform into the arms of other children below just as adults had done in the performances of *Paradise Now*.

When someone complained to the authorities, eighteen members of the company were arrested and charged with possession of marijuana which was said to have been found in their garden. They had been in Ouro Preto only five months, but the Living Theatre had forgotten a lesson learned in Europe – if they stayed in one locale more than two months they would be harrassed in one way or another. They knew from the nature of their work, their life-style, and their political convictions that they must keep moving. In Brazil they made a tactical error and they paid for it by spending two months in prison before they were deported.

Back in the United States the company continued to develop the *Legacy of Cain* cycle and to devote their energies to industrial workers. They lent support to various industrial organizing activities and in so far as possible they followed their principle of staying outside the money system, but it was necessary to raise money through lectures and workshops. They created, for performances to academic communities, *Seven Meditations on Political Sado-Masochism* (1973) which they considered a 'study piece' on the 'manifestation of the sado-masochist syndrome in various aspects of our lives'.[14]

They received a grant from the Mellon Foundation to produce theatre in Pittsburgh, where they moved at the end of 1974 and began working with coal miners, steel mill workers, and their families. They set out to use their theatre skills to focus the attention of these workers on their condition and to stimulate discussion to help bring about social, political, and economic change that would result in the workers taking control of production and replacing the profit motive with a creative impulse in their work.[15]

While in Pittsburgh they produced two major plays for *The Legacy of Cain* cycle, also on the theme of the master/slave relationship which they believe to be the basis of all relationships in our society. The first of these plays, *Six Public Acts to Transmute Violence into Concord: Tampering with the Master/Slave System: Ceremonies and Processions: Changing Pittsburgh: Prologue to 'The Legacy of Cain'* (May 1975), again uses the six houses of enslavement. After gathering in one place the spectators move in a procession to six locations in the city and six ceremonial events are presented. The first stop is The House of Death represented by a utility company building. Performers enact the agony of death, other performers remove the shoes of the victims and line them up in front of the spectators. Then, as in *Mysteries*, the rigid corpses are put into a pile. At a public flag pole which represents The House of State, each of the performers pricks a finger and smears blood on the flag pole while commemorating an act of the state which has resulted in deaths. In front of a bank, The House of Money, money is burned and fake-bills are distributed to the spectators. Each bill carries the statement: 'Whoever accepts money is the slave of the government who prints it.' Outside a highrise apartment house, The House of Property, the performers erect a two-tiered jail-like structure reminiscent of that used in *Frankenstein*. Simultaneously they sing 'Who built this building? Who built the pyramids?' etcetera. The ceremony for The House of War is enacted in front of the local police station. 'This is the house of our brothers. Flesh and blood like ours.' Bread and roses are given to the police or left for them if they do not appear. In a park, The House of Love, the actors recite a poem on the theme of love as a struggle for possession in the master/slave relationship.

Throughout the performance of *Six Public Acts* real time and place, and therefore the integration of the performance with life, were emphasized in several ways. In walking from place to place spectators could not help but be aware of real space. Furthermore, they were made to focus on actual buildings rather than theatrical scenery and to think about the building in relation to the real world. Finally, every fifteen seconds throughout the entire performance, an actor playing the Shaman of Time (Death) announced the actual clock time.

The Money Tower (1975), the second Pittsburgh play, focuses on one of the houses of enslavement analysing the enslaving power of money. It was presented in several locations including outside the gates of a steel mill as workers were changing shifts. A tower is erected eleven metres tall with five acting levels, graphically demonstrating the position of the worker in the capitalist society. At the very top is a dollar, then the elite, next the church/state/law/ military establishment, then the bourgeoisie, the workers, and at the very bottom the poor and the unemployed. The design was borrowed in part from Mayakovsky's 1930 production of *Moscow Is Burning,* and the construction of the tower was similar to that in *Frankenstein.* The tower depicts the conversion of ore into money as sacks of material are conveyed from the bottom of the structure to the top. The ore is pulled up by the workers and processed into ingots by the working class, on the next level the middle class regulates production, further up the police and law establishment guards the precious metal, and finally it reaches the elite who accumulate the money in a bank. A portion of the money is sent down the tower in the form of wages which are then reaccumulated by the elite in the form of payments for rent, products, food, and taxes. This is followed by a section in which the visions of the poor and working class are the nightmares of the rich. In the final section the ruling class want more money so they demand lower wages, longer hours, and layoffs. A strike and rebellion develop and a violent confrontation with the Army/Police seems inevitable, but a happy ending is provided as the people discuss bringing into being an anarchistic society which functions without money.

The Living Theatre had been undergoing another major transition. Not only did they give up performing in theatres, they gave up the confrontational method influenced by Artaud. Instead of the aggressive tone of *Paradise Now,* they wanted audience participation on a co-operative basis. And instead of the isolated super-individualistic approach, they attempted to learn about the problems and perspectives of their potential audiences. They participated in local progressive organizations and helped form food co-operatives. They invited spectators to visit them for informal discussions. In short the Living Theatre attempted to become a model of the anarchistic society. 'Our presence is our message,' said Beck, 'we are what we stand for.'[16] Their rehearsal methods became more collective. Malina and Beck still had the greatest impact on the productions, but rehearsals were now conducted without a director which, although less efficient, demonstrated that work could be accomplished without bosses. They were encouraged by the interest in their performances, especially since they had been warned that they would be greeted by apathy and rejection. They discovered, however, that they could not survive in the United States outside the economic system. Having given up theatres they had also given up their income. And as they had said in *Paradise Now,* 'You can't live if you don't have money.'

In the autumn of 1975 they accepted invitations and fees to perform at several European festivals including the Biennale in Venice. In Italy they found a volatile changing culture where municipal Communist governments were interested in using the arts to increase social and economic awareness. There was a keen interest in libertarian alternatives and they thought 'perhaps in this country something could actually happen'.[17] Furthermore provinces and cities were willing to subsidize performances. They made Rome their headquarters but toured throughout the country sponsored by schools, factories, unions, psychiatric hospitals and performing in the streets, gymnasiums, schools and other non-theatrical spaces. *Six Public Acts* proved popular for such venues.

They also began performing again in theatres and on the theatre circuits in Italy and other European countries. While working exclusively with the culturally and educationally disadvantaged, there was little opportunity for interaction with the intellectual community. By re-entering the ambiance of theatre they could again participate in the 'moral, philosophical, social, psychological dialogue . . . taking place among those who have the social advantage of education'. They had become less hostile in their 'view of those who sustain the system because of social pressures'. According to Malina, during their years of street theatre they had learned to respect their audience.

Prometheus (1978) was collectively created for performance in theatres. It is a symbolic intellectual work using ideas from previous productions and introducing in the second act a new technique for involving spectators in the performance. As the title suggests, the play is concerned with the ways in which humans have been bound – physically, spiritually, and culturally. The setting is dominated by a large arch constructed of pipe. When the audience enters, performers are discovered bound with ropes in theatre seats. The performance begins when spectators untie them. Act One presents a dream-like history of culture using historical and mythological figures. It is a history of increasing confinement. The creative inventiveness of the anarchistic Prometheus (Hanon Reznikov), symbolized by his bringing fire to mankind, is punished by Zeus (Julian Beck) representing the forces of order. A chorus of doctors including Aristotle and Pythagoras discover various geometric shapes which bring order, but when each shape is placed on the head of an actor, he is overwhelmed. Zeus suppresses women's wisdom and incorporates it by swallowing Metis (Imke Buchholz). The belly of Zeus is represented by a prison where Metis is confined. Through the telescope of Metis Zeus sees the devout Io (Judith Malina) who is transformed into a cow pursued by the furies. The style of the first act is similar to their work of the late sixties – shouting, demonstrable speech rather than representational acting, nude and semi-nude bodies.

The style of Act Two is epic realism. The events surrounding the Russian Revolution are enacted by members of the company with the help of spectator volunteers. The script is primarily from the writings of the historical participants, but dramatic license is taken with chronology. For example, the act begins with the simultaneous arrival in Russia of Lenin (Beck) in 1917 and the anarchists Emma Goldman (Malina) and Alexander Berkman (Reznikov) in 1920. When the anarchists ask why fellow anarchists are being kept in prison, Lenin replies: 'Free speech is a bourgeois luxury . . . a tool of reaction.'

The rest of Act Two (about sixty-five minutes) is the re-enactment of the storming of the Winter Palace. Lenin/Beck gives a short illustrated lecture on the event using a map. He asks for volunteers to play four bolsheviks, ten-to-twelve anarchists, three-to-four Tolstoyan pacifists, four terrorists,

9. *Prometheus*

five women in jail, two actors in Mayakovsky's troupe, Red Guards, infantrymen, etc. Each group rehearses with a company member. Some are given scripts of their slogans and actions. Four red tapes are stretched across the stage indicating the entrance to the palace. Lenin/Beck, at a lectern, narrates the action and gives historical speeches from time to time. Some of the actions of volunteers involve charging the palace with guns (rolled-up paper) firing (drums). At the end of each charge Lenin/Beck orders one of the red tapes to be cut. The Tolstoyan pacifists cross the stage cutting imaginary wheat while making swishing sounds. At one point everyone in the audience is involved as they are asked to perform emblematic gestures. Lenin is asked, 'If a worker has to work for sixteen hours a day, is he free?' Lenin replies, 'No!' but disdainfully refuses to answer when asked, 'If a worker has to work eight hours a day, is he free?' A woman describes how free women are after the revolution as she is bound up with a red cloth. Eventually, Lenin dies and is lifted to the top of a pyramid, the Living Theatre's symbol of hierarchical oppression. A scene from Mayakovsky's *Moscow is Burning* is performed with biomechanics, a gymnastic style of acting which the bolshevik

32

10. *Prometheus*

playwright–director had invented. However, Mayakovsky becomes disillusioned and shoots himself.

When the lights come up for Act Three the entire company is hanging by arms and legs, motionless, from the metal pipe scaffolding. After a time Julian Beck says, 'The scene is Prometheus unbound, a silent action. We will go to Holloway Prison [in the London performance] and there to perform an act of meditation – a five-minute vigil in the name of the end of punishment.' Those who wish go to the prison with the company to perform a vigil. A programme note for this act says, 'The question is: for what crime, if any, are we being punished when we are being punished?'

In the view of Julian Beck Acts One and Two tell the same story. They demonstrate how human consciousness has been contained within a pyramidal structure of conceptualization which is intrinsically hierarchical and patriarchal. In Act One the structure is represented by Zeus and the pantheon of gods as well as the historical progenitors of knowledge and culture. Against this structure Prometheus represents the creative self which wants to be free. This pattern is repeated in Act Two through the presentation of the Russian Revolution, which Malina considers the modern myth to which everyone is bound. The ideal of the communist revolution, according to Beck, had been the breaking away from a pyramidal social structure and replacing it with a more decentralized and less authoritarian structure. Unfortunately, it resulted in a re-establishment of 'an authoritarian pyramidal form which ultimately leads to the prison or Prometheus bound on the rock'. In the second act Lenin is the patriarchal figure and the anarchists Goldman and Berkman are the persecuted freedom seekers. Beck thinks of the first two acts as two dreams which tell the same story with different incidents. They are also conceived as a parallel to the first two parts of the Aeschylean trilogy – *Prometheus the Fire Bringer* and *Prometheus Bound*. The third act relates to *Prometheus Unbound*, the third play in the Greek trilogy. However, the unbinding must take place in the spectator's head. Going to a prison carries the action into the street and permits the spectator to project the classical and modern mythology upon the architecture of our time. For Beck, 'Standing in front of a prison is to say that all of history has led to this brick wall. There is nothing to do but look and think about it. The objective of the play is to bring about this meditation in the spectator'.

The process of collectively developing *Prometheus* began with discussions concerning the subject and theme of the play and progressed to research on Greek mythology and psychological images. As always, the guiding principle was that the individual should not be sacrificed to the collective nor the collective to the individual. In attempts to find a structure for the play they decided that each actor would choose a character from classical mythology or a historical figure that would relate to the myth. For example, Beck chose Zeus because of his interest in overcoming the pyramidal power structure which crushes those on the bottom. Bucholz chose to play Metis because of her concern with the suppression of female knowledge and the imprisonment of women. Once the characters were chosen, the plot of the first act was developed around the roles. Then Beck had the idea (Act Two) of translating the Promethean myth into the historical myth, and they searched for analogous characters associated with the Russian Revolution. Each of them asked the question in relation to their Act One character – If so-and-so had been in the Revolution who would she/he have been? Zeus became Lenin, Prometheus became the imprisoned Alexander Berkman, Metis became an anarchist prisoner and a feminist. Judith Malina, who had played Io pursued by the furies in Act One, became the anarchist Emma Goldman in Act Two. The actress saw a parallel not only to 'the wandering, driven spirit of Io' but to her own biography – 'an exile, wandering, deported and pursued, nowhere at home'.

From the beginning the Living Theatre have adhered to an anarchist objective and have practised their message as much as they have preached it. But while their objective has remained constant, Judith Malina points out that their perspective has changed. 'We try to remain cognizant of the stream of history so as to stay valid within it. This means a constant change of vocabulary, form, and vision.'

In the course of their search for means to articulate their relation to a dynamic present, they invented or adapted nearly every experimental concept associated with the alternative theatre of the sixties and seventies. They were one of the first groups to explore the unique possibilities of live performers in relation to the spectators in their presence. Developing that relationship became important for the Living Theatre because it was a prerequisite to helping the spectator to a spiritual change which ultimately could lead to the desired change in society. They developed a variety of means to keep the audience focused on real time and place so as to make possible an actor/spectator relationship. They attempted to shock the spectators into reality to help them break through the culturally-imposed restrictions on their feelings and actions. In *The Brig* they developed an acting style which they did not consider representation but 'a state of being' because the performer actually experienced what was being enacted. Beginning with *Mysteries* actors wore their own everyday clothes, sometimes played themselves rather than fictional characters, confronted the audience aggressively, used actual exercises in their performances, and permitted spectators to participate. Actors were not restricted to the stage nor spectators to the auditorium. In order to focus on the presence of the performer, actors played several roles, they remained in view throughout the performance, and there was an attempt to eliminate the rational impediment between impulse and reaction. The body and voice were used expressionistically. Through suggestive actions and sounds the physical setting used in *Franken-stein* became a ship, the world, prison cells, or the head of the Creature. With their voices and bodies the actors created the necessary sound effects. Through abstract miming and acrobatics they suggested fire in *Frankenstein* and spelled out words in *Paradise Now*. They encouraged the audience to participate in a group embrace which became so popular in *Paradise Now*, and later in *Dionysus in 69* by the Performance Group, that it was given the sarcastic epithet of 'group grope'. One-third of *Paradise Now* – the 'Action' sections – was not planned but left to the spectators and performers to develop through their own spontaneous actions. In parts of some performances the company functioned more as group therapists or recreation leaders than as traditional actors. All of these techniques and others served to focus on the live performer in the here and now rather than absorbing the spectator's psyche into a fictional illusion of character, time, and place. In short, the audience was made to focus on the real world.

For the Living Theatre life is theatre and theatre is their life. Beginning with *Mysteries,* they became primarily interested in presenting reality rather than fiction. It was expected that actors joining the company would fit into the committed, nomadic, anarchistic community which existed entirely to present themselves as theatre. 'Acting is not make believe', said one of the performers, 'but living exquisitely in the moment.'[18] In principle, the performance was built of the actors' experiences in probing within themselves. Although some members practised yoga or various psycho-physical exercises, there was no need for special training. Anyone can perform. All that is necessary, according to Beck, is 'an atmosphere in which the individual is free to create . . . to draw upon his own resources'. The Living Theatre community intended to promote this sense of freedom. They tended to avoid institutionalized relationships within the company and to practise sexual freedom. Although Beck and Malina were married, they came to believe that the institution of marriage was an extension of the concept of ownership, loved one as property, which produced jealousy when domination was threatened. They eschewed institutionalized politics as this led to bureaucracy and repression. Because the mind and the body had been conditioned to restrictions by our culture, drugs could be used to release the mind and nudity could help free the body. It was hoped that by throwing off artificial restrictions their lives would become unified, they would break out of the compartmentalized structure of society which tended to fragment people's lives into work, recreation, family, religion, politics, etc.

In principle they avoided a company structure as this would tend to institutionalize a hierarchy, but members of the company received programme credit for specific responsibilities including Malina and/or Beck as directors of the productions. However, Beck said in 1969 that 'the real work of the director in the modern theatre is to eliminate himself' or 'at least to establish inside the acting company a situation in which the actor is . . . able to take more and more control of the total work'.[19] Although some members of the company contributed more to a production than others, beginning with *Mysteries* nearly all the productions were created collectively. In general the collective process involved discussion, improvisation, and research. Beck and Malina continued to provide the over-all view, the structuring of the works, and whatever writing was required.

The techniques they used over the years comprise a catalogue of nearly all the techniques associated with the alternative theatre in Europe and America. In many of the later productions the action was non-linear. They used language collage in *Frankenstein* and other plays. The concept of chance was explored in *The Marrying Maiden*. Improvisation in performance became common. In *The Connection* and other plays they experimented with the ambivalence of fiction and reality. They created productions inspired by other literary sources such as *Frankenstein*. In nearly all of the plays beginning with *Mysteries* there were opportunities for the physical participation of spectators. In Brazil, Pittsburgh, and Italy they set out to find a new audience of industrial workers, and some works were informed by discussions with this audience. *Six Public Acts* used the technique of a peripatetic audience and actual places were used instead of scenery.

The Living Theatre had begun in 1951 with an attempt to resuscitate poetic language in the theatre, but by the mid-sixties they had de-emphasized words in keeping with the dominant tendency of alternative theatre. This was practical as they were playing in countries where different languages were spoken, but after creating *Paradise Now* Beck discussed another reason. The object was not to destroy language, said Beck, but to reach toward a 'kind of communication of feeling and idea . . . that is beneath words or beyond words, or *in addition to words*' 'Words are too rational. They lead people to accept knowledge but avoid experience.'[20]

Various of the techniques introduced or adapted by the Living Theatre became formulated into theatrical modes of the sixties and seventies. It can be said that Malina and Beck explored more of these modes than any other company, although they were not the pioneers in each of these. In many of their productions there were elements from *Happenings*. Some of their work can be considered *Political Theatre* in that it was concerned with social and economic problems. Many of their later productions were *Street Theatre,* being performed out-of-doors, going to the audience rather than the audience coming to them. Some of the work in Brazil was *Guerrilla Theatre* (a term popularized by R.G. Davis of the San Francisco Mime Troupe) in that they arrived at a site unexpectedly, performed illegally, and could get away quickly. In some of their productions the performers and spectators occupied the same space and there were several simultaneous focuses, important characteristics of *Environmental Theatre* which have been explored in greatest depth by Richard Schechner, the founder of the Performance Group.

The Living Theatre have been influenced by Meyerhold, Piscator, Artaud, and Brecht, but there has also been a reciprocal influence with some of their contemporaries – especially Grotowski and his Polish Laboratory Theatre, Peter Schumann and the Bread and Puppet Theater, Joseph Chaikin and the Open Theatre. And the Living Theatre have had an important impact upon younger theatre companies, some formed with the Living Theatre as their model and others making use of their techniques. These included in France Orbe–Récherche théâtrale, Théâtre du chêne noir, Tréteau libre; in England C.A.S.T., Red Ladder Theatre, The Freehold, T.O.C.; in the United States the Firehouse Theatre, The Company Theatre, Alive and Trucking. Fewer than half of these were still functioning in 1980.

In 1980 the Living Theatre was thirty years old, which probably makes it the oldest American theatre company of any kind. Surely it is the only existing theatre to have adhered to its ideals so tenaciously in the face of such hardships. Suffering ridicule, poverty, a nomadic life, deportation, and imprisonment they have continued their dedication to a spiritual revolution which they hope will bring about a revolution in social, economic, and political structures. Against the repression they saw in our culture they juxtaposed their experimental art as a non-violent challenge and their anarchistic community as a model of the better world which could exist. Judith Malina and Julian Beck held fast to their convictions as times changed – as the commitments of the counter-culture in the sixties dissolved in youthful opportunism in the seventies, as the pacifism of the sixties transformed into disillusionment or in some instances violence in the early seventies and indifference at the end of the decade. At all times there were those who ridiculed the Living Theatre – even other revolutionaries who were prepared to exchange one violent oppressive system for another. For some others, Beck and Malina were martyrs and attending a performance was akin to a religious experience. The Living Theatre lifted a responsibility from their shoulders by doing on their behalf what they lacked the commitment to do themselves.

The Open Theatre

More than any other theatre in the late 1960s the Open Theatre furthered the concept of collective creation. The company, under the direction of Joseph Chaikin, borrowed, adapted, and invented psycho-physical exercises which served as the chief means of creating material. By the time the Open Theatre disbanded in 1973 after ten years of work, the training exercises associated with them had come to be used by many other theatre groups in the United States and Europe as a means of creating their own productions.

When Chaikin formed the Open Theatre in 1963 it was to provide a workshop for theatre exploration rather than performance. Beginning in 1959 Chaikin had been an actor in the Living Theatre, the only experimental theatre in New York at that time. He was interested in finding a theatrical expression other than realism and in exploring the unique possibilities of live theatre as distinct from television and cinema. Eventually this led Chaikin to develop the concept of 'presence'. In the work of the Open Theatre the performer was in focus – not the character.

Chaikin came to refer to the 'outside' and the 'inside' of a situation. Realistic behaviour was the outside, and it was this which the conventional theatre presented in its productions. Chaikin was interested in discovering the inside through abstract non-verbal improvisations. The first performances by the new theatre consisted of these improvisations and exercises, some of which were structured into short pieces by playwrights Jean-Claude van Itallie and Megan Terry.

The first long play developed improvisationally was *Viet Rock,* presented at Cafe La Mama in 1966. Megan Terry had been conducting a weekly Open Theatre workshop. the anger of Terry and the workshop participants toward the involvement of the United States in the Vietnam war resulted in improvisations on the theme of violence. Using a variety of sources dealing with the war – newspapers, eyewitness accounts, letters – as the basis for improvisations, they developed material which was then structured by Megan Terry. The group met every day for the two or three weeks prior to performance when Chaikin helped with some of the staging.

The finished work was a collage of transformations unified by the theme of war and a loose chronological structure dealing with young men who are inducted into the army, trained, sent to Vietnam to fight, and are killed. The sixteen actors in the production change character frequently and sometimes are inanimate objects or simply themselves. The continuity is that of the presence of the performers rather than of specific characters. No scenery is used, the actors wear their own clothes, and there are few props.

The actors enter while a recording of the song 'The Viet Rock' is playing. They lie on their backs with their heads together forming a circle. Gradually movement can be detected, then sounds of humming, babies gurgling, childlike sounds of laughter, sounds of children playing war games, cowboys and

11. *Viet Rock*, **photo: Open Theatre**

Indians, cops and robbers. The sounds build to a climax and the performers rise holding hands. They circle around and are flung to different parts of the stage. The men are transformed into babies and the women become mothers who kneel beside the nearest baby. The only words they speak are 'mama' and 'baby'. One actor is transformed into the Sergeant. He jumps to his feet, yells orders and the male performers become men who form lines. The women become doctors who examine the men for induction into the army. Later the women form an aeroplane and make aeroplane sounds as they fly the men to Vietnam. The story of American soldiers in Vietnam unfolds – one of the men is wounded and dies, the men dance with Vietnamese women in a bar, and at the end everyone is killed in an explosion. After a period of silence, disjointed phrases referring to violence, war, and religion are heard from the pile of bodies in the centre of the stage. Then the performers go into the audience, each chooses a spectator and touches his or her hand, head, face, and hair. The group refers to this action as 'a celebration of presence'. It is an expression of what Chaikin considers the distinctive possibility of theatre as compared with cinema or television or the absorbing fictional world of the realistic theatre. It is the immediacy, the existential encounter which the live actor makes possible. He believes that the ultimate value of the theatre is the confrontation of the spectators with the mortality they share – 'the visceral confrontation with the reality that one is living now and at some other time no longer living'.[21]

Although direct confrontation was not used again, other means of accentuating the presence of the performer were used in all subsequent work. Actors did not wear costumes to identify them as specific characters, even though special clothing was worn. By playing the 'inside' of a situation, actors did not play realistic characters which would mask them from the audience. And movement and speech were not representational in style but abstracted, so that they tended to indicate or demonstrate.

In autumn 1967 Chaikin and a group of actors began using the Book of Genesis as a focus for discussions and improvisations. The psycho-physical exercises continued with renewed commitment because of a visit by Jerzy Grotowski who was working with similar exercises in his Laboratory Theatre. The Open Theatre workshop met four days a week for four hours, and van Itallie took the responsibility of giving structure to the work being evolved. When completed *The Serpent* included places for the group to improvise in performance. In addition to biblical images, the finished non-linear transformational work includes images from the assassinations of President Kennedy and Martin Luther King. However, most of the scenes derive from the Book of Genesis.

As women in the chorus echo Eve's thoughts, the five-man serpent leads Eve to the choice of eating the apple. She takes a couple of frantic bites, savours her experience, then goes to Adam and persuades him to eat. When Adam has tasted the apple, all of the actors, in a kind of ecstasy, form the serpent. The serpent separates and the actors take apples from a bag, eat them, and carry them to the audience. Adam can neither swallow the bite he has taken nor spit it out. Adam is pulled up by his arms and speaks for God when God is speaking to Adam.

In the Cain and Abel scene Cain wants to kill his brother but he does not know this will cause his death. Cain does not know how to kill. He pulls at Abel, lifts him up, chops at him with his hands. When Abel stops breathing, Cain tries to breathe breath back into him with his own mouth, he tries to stand him up, he wants Abel to be alive again. At the end of the play they walk through the audience and leave the theatre.

While the plays which followed were developed by much the same method as *The Serpent*, the starting points were somewhat different. Each of the last three plays began with an exploration of a universal human concern.

Terminal (1969) evolved out of a collective investigation into human mortality and a consideration of both personal and societal responses to the fact of death. Directors Joe Chaikin and Roberta Sklar and the group of eighteen performers prepared for work on the new play by reading David Cooper's *Death in the Family* and the prison letters of black radical George Jackson. An embalmer explained how people are embalmed, and the description became a part of the production. Joseph Campbell talked about death in mythology, and the performers themselves collected ideas and improvised on their dreams and on specific characters. Susan Yankowitz, who was responsible for the text, joined the workshop at a later stage to observe, to help focus ideas, and to create original material which would elucidate the themes.

12. *The Serpent*, **photo: Open Theatre**

Terminal was first performed in Europe, touring to France, Switzerland and West Germany. When they returned to the United States there were serious frictions within the group. Some believed the Open Theatre should be primarily a social community while others believed the primary purpose of the group should be theatrical exploration. They disbanded, and after a few months Chaikin re-formed the group with only six performers. Raymond Barry, Shami Chaikin, Ellen Maddow, Jo Ann Schmidman, Tina Shepard, and Paul Zimet were chosen for their skill in carrying on the theatrical explorations of the Open Theatre. The performances of *Terminal* resumed.[22]

The only scenery used in the production is small rolling platforms of various heights, a clothing rack, a ladder, several stools, and large pieces of plywood. These props serve as beds, embalming tables, walls, and graves. The actors wear simple white garments and play a number of roles – hospital attendants, wardens, embalmers, and the dying. As in other Open Theatre productions there is much use of percussive sound, in this case most often produced by body percussion.

13. *Terminal*

Each segment of the play is announced by one or more actors.[23] The performance begins with 'The Calling up of the Dead'. The performers call upon the dead to speak through them, the dying. 'Let them take my body, let them use my tongue.' The actors change from street clothes to white costumes. They are alive, but they are dying. In 'The Last Biological Rites', an actor faces the audience, an anonymous attendant at his side who says without feeling, 'This is your last chance to use your eyes.' The actor tries to see to the utmost, but his vision fails. The attendant gives him pieces of black tape with which the blind man seals off his eyes. The actor makes sounds but his voice fades and he can no longer speak. He is given a piece of black tape and he puts it over his mouth. The attendant says, 'This is your last chance to use your legs.' The actor stumbles forward, his legs give way, and he falls to his knees. The attendant lifts him onto a small low platform. His only remaining visible sign of life is his breathing.

The actors perform 'The Dance on the Graves of the Dead'. At various points throughout the play one of the dead inhabits the body of an actor as when the Soldier speaks through the actor's mouth. The actor marches in place saluting to the rhythm of the march as she repeats 'Dead because I said "Yes", dead because you said "Yes".' In another segment, 'Cosmetics', three performers makeup, transforming themselves into artificial-looking people. In 'The Interview' the person being interviewed is forced to remove

14. *Terminal*

all his clothes in exchange for the white hospital uniform. He is also measured for his coffin and his photograph is taken so his appearance can be restored when he dies. Another of the dead, the Executed Man, tells the audience they are condemned to death like him. Another performer holds a piece of plywood upright, rocking it from side to side making a rhythmic knocking sound. 'The Dying Imagine Their Judgment' is the concluding section. The judge, using a megaphone, reads the judgements as the other performers act out appropriate images.

The judgment of your life is your life.
You will finally possess the thing you wanted most in life – and eternity
will be that thing and that thing only.

. . .

43

> You neither faced your death nor participated in your life, but straddled
> the line between one place and the other, longing for both.
> The judgment of your life is your life.
> . . .
> You are standing in a space filled with bodies and you watch their
> couplings and breathe their odors, but you cannot touch them and
> they will not reach out to you.

At the end of the performance the actors stand silently; the focus is on the relationship between the spectators and performers who are in each other's presence, on the moment which is passing as all move inevitably toward death. The performance has shown up our cultural tendency to make the death of others relevant while obscuring the fact that we ourselves are dying.

Their next production, *The Mutation Show* (1971), grew out of workshops on another universal human quality. The unifying theme was the adaptation of people to various circumstances which tend to transform them into social freaks. In preparing the work the group drew upon some of the same sources they had used for *Terminal* and they also studied mythology and rites of change – puberty rites, marriage ceremonies, funerals – practised in various cultures. They became interested in Kaspar Hauser, the early nineteenth-century German boy who spent the first sixteen years of his life in a cellar removed from the influence of society. The members of the Open Theatre asked themselves and each other questions such as 'Who do you see when you look at me? What do you think I see when I look at you?' According to Chaikin, who with Roberta Sklar directed the workshops, these questions were intended to bring the group to a kind of crisis so as to release the work.

As in their other collective work, *The Mutation Show* made use of performer-produced sound–non-verbal vocal sounds, percussion created by body and feet. But they also played tom tom, tambourine, drum, cymbals, sliding whistles, wooden flutes, accordion, washboard, and home-made instruments. Most of the music was developed improvisationally.

The structure of the play is that of a circus controlled by a ringmaster (Shami Chaikin) who announces the scenes and participates in them. She introduces each of the performers as one of the characters they play during the show. They project personalities which society has imposed upon them or which have resulted from their adaptations to the expectations of society. In part the traits assumed by the performers are based on an aspect of their own personality which they came to recognize during the course of the workshops. Tom Lillard, dressed in a football jersey, smiles continuously. Jo Ann Schmidman, announced as the Bird Lady, prances around the stage. Raymond Barry is introduced as the Man Who Hits Himself on the Head, which he does regularly. Tina Shepard is the Thinker; she wanders around the stage trying to think. Paul Zimet is the Petrified Man. Each character has his or her own vocal sounds suggesting a pre-language state where the distinction between human and animal is unclear.

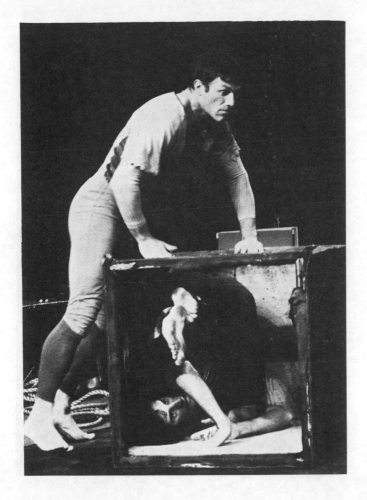

15.   *The Mutation Show*

The Ringmaster introduces the next character who is derived from Kaspar Hauser. 'The Boy in the Box. He lived alone in his box all his life . . . One Day he was torn from his box and carried to a hill where he was left.' The boy is curled up in the box as in a womb. As Ray Barry pulls him from the box he makes frightened animal sounds. The boy attaches himself to his abductor's back, and the man walks in place, swaying from side to side, panting in time with his steps. The boy holds tightly around the man's neck, sometimes strangling him, and the man must push his arms away. From time to time the boy makes animal cries as he sways from side to side countering the movements of the man carrying him. At the end of the journey, the man struggles to untangle the boy from his back and eventually succeeds, leaving him on the ground.

16. *The Mutation Show*

The Ringmaster introduces 'The Animal Girl. She ate and drank and slept with an animal pack. One day she was torn from her cage and taken away and made civilized.' The Animal Girl cries and screeches as she is roped by a hunter. The Ringmaster explains 'We will name her. We will give her words. We will straighten her bones. We will caress her.' As this is repeated over and over the girl's legs are straightened, her feet are put into a pair of high-heeled shoes, and her legs are made to walk as she is held in an upright position. Finally she walks on her own. She has adapted.

In the section called The Weddings the performers are pairs of lovers adapting to each other and to society. Music plays and a man and a woman come forward smiling to show the world how happy they are. A man-as-master and a woman-as-dog come forward. Two men are holding hands but looking innocently away from each other. A man and a woman come

17. *The Mutation Show*

forward, she with a bicycle horn between her legs which her friend beeps by reaching behind her and squeezing the bulb. Each time he beeps, she is startled and then looks at him coyly.

In The Wedding Dance which follows, the performers dance as the Musician plays a small accordion and announces 'The groom is now dancing with the mother of the bride . . . The father of the groom is now dancing with the Captain of Police . . . The butcher is now dancing with the people . . . The earth is now dancing with the stars.'

The six performers line up across the stage holding large photographs of themselves from other periods in their lives and the Musician gives a brief biography of each. Through the observable changes in their appearance and their histories the audience gains insights into the adaptations they have made to people, places, periods, and events. The performers, like the characters they have been demonstrating, are social mutants.

47

18. *The Mutation Show*

The theme of social mutation had been in Chaikin's mind for some time. He has commented several years earlier on how people modify themselves because of a desire to succeed in the theatre. The more you adapt, he said, the less you know yourself. You lose a connection to your real responses. Chaikin sought to avoid this kind of adaptation in forming the Open Theatre. The workshops, unlike training for the commercial theatre, would not try to make the actors 'better commodities'. The purpose of the Open Theatre was not so much the creation of a product, but investigation through theatre of certain forces in our culture and an attempt to invent the means necessary to express and share the actors' insights through performance. As their reputation grew the pressures to remain the same increased. They had a reputation to protect. Furthermore, by continuing to do similar work there was a probability of increased financial rewards. Chaikin and some others felt they were being seduced by these pressures and the group decided to disband. Ironically, it was not possible for the Open Theatre to remain the same and still be the Open Theatre. The purpose of the theatre was exploration and change.

They made one more play, but it was still considered a work-in-progress, not having been enriched by continuous improvements over an extended period of performances. *Nightwalk* (1973), like previous plays, dealt with universal human conditions, in this case sleep and consciousness, both physical and social. However, *Terminal* and *The Mutation Show* were the most mature and complex works created by the Open Theatre.

The Open Theatre was open and deliberately eclectic. Chaikin had trained as a Method actor, but the Open Theatre was also influenced by Brecht, Artaud, the Living Theatre, Grotowski, Peter Brook, Viola Spolin, and, no doubt, by everyone who worked with it. Eclecticism is typical of the alternative theatres in general, and Chaikin made it a strength through his ability to select and assimilate those ideas and practices which served its needs.

Of all the groups in the United States, the Open Theatre most nearly paralleled Grotowski's Theatre Laboratory in its search for the distinctive elements of theatre and in its physical and vocal discipline. It adapted some of Grotowski's psycho-physical exercises as well as those from other sources such as Spolin. The exercises, according to Chaikin, provided a 'common ground for those who study together'. Furthermore, they provided structures for improvisation, which was the chief means used by the group to develop their plays. It was through improvisation that the performer shared with the playwright and the director the responsibility for the artistic conception. The collective creation of a work in this manner requires much more energy and time than the conventional method of writing a script and staging it. Discovering ways of working together intimately without destructive friction, and concentrating sufficiently to stave off enervating boredom, requires persistent energy.

Chaikin came to believe that a writer could provide an important ingredient in collective work that otherwise would be lacking, and he attempted to incorporate a writer into the group for each of the collectively created works. However, he thinks he never found a satisfactory way of working with a writer in the collective situation. Although writers participated to varying degrees in the creation of *The Serpent, Terminal,* and *The Mutation Show,* the importance of the writer seemed to decrease with each production.

All of the collective plays beginning with *The Serpent* toured extensively in the United States and Europe. These performances and the exercises disseminated by the Open Theatre influenced theatre groups on both continents in the late 1960s and the 1970s. Nearly every institution which trains actors uses exercises developed or adapted by the Open Theatre. But the principle which chiefly distinguished Chaikin's work was that the performer was always in focus – not a character as in realistic theatre. His concept of acting is based upon the idea that the uniqueness of live theatre is the encounter between live performers and spectators.

3
Theatre of Social Change

Many theatre groups formed in the sixties and seventies reflect social movements. As with the movements themselves, these theatres aim to bring about social change. Some are content to change attitudes and raise the morale of their constituent audiences, others promote acceptance by the dominant culture, and others would change society, equalizing economic and social benefits. A few groups do not represent an identifiable ethnic or social movement, but attempt to raise political consciousness by presenting in their work a socialist analysis of American society. The Living Theatre has provided one model for making theatre with a social efficacy. Other models had existed in the workers' theatres during the depression years of the 1930s. And Brecht's plays and theoretical writings were especially important for demonstrating an aesthetic involving social analysis.

Among the new groups who see themselves as reviving the workers' theatre concept, the most important is the San Francisco Mime Troupe. There are other groups, however, with less doctrinaire political views who feel an affinity with workers in a capitalist society – especially blue-collar workers – and present in their plays a discussion of their economic problems. During the Vietnam War, however, most of these groups focused their work on raising audience consciousness of horrors being perpetrated upon South East Asia by the United States.

The Provisional Theatre formed as a collective in Los Angeles in 1972. Their first work, *Xa: A Vietnam Primer*, is a history of the people of Vietnam. It is performed on a large map of Vietnam outlined on the floor with tape. In alternating scenes the performers speak directly to the audience as themselves or read a narrative history of Vietnam while others, using dance-like

19.   Xa: A Vietnam Primer, photo: Provisional Theatre

movement, act out the various armies and rearrange the tape as borders change. The acting style emphasizes body movement and vocal sounds based on Open Theatre exercises. A later production, *Inching Through the Everglades* (1978), is an idealistic play with songs about working people in America – their self-image, frustrations, and isolation. The characters tell their own stories directly to the audience, touching on themes of racism, sexism, loneliness, and growing old.

The first of the black theatres of the 1960s was the Free Southern Theatre formed in 1963 by Gilbert Moses and John O'Neal as part of the civil rights movement in Mississippi. Their aim was to develop a theatre which would reflect the cultural experience of blacks. They hoped to develop self-esteem among their black audiences; by presenting plays with historical and social analysis they intended to educate their audiences to the causes of their oppression and indicate means for alleviating it. The objectives of other black theatres were much the same, although the emphasis varied. In 1966 The Negro Ensemble Company was formed in New York by Douglas Turner Ward, Robert Hooks, and Gerald S. Krone for the additional purpose of providing continual training and performance opportunities for black theatre artists who were ignored by the Broadway and Off-Broadway theatres. The early plays, such as *Ceremonies in Dark Old Men* (1969) by Lonne Elder III, dealt with the problems of black people as victims in society. In the early 1970s productions such as *The Black Terror* focused on black–white conflicts and showed the black man as a revolutionary. By the mid-1970s the plays were concerned with more universal problems, such as family loyalty in *In the Deepest Part of Sleep* (1974) by Charles Fuller. The New Lafayette Theatre, founded in 1967 by playwright Ed Bullins and director Robert Macbeth, was conceived as a theatre for Harlem, New York City's black ghetto. Until it closed in 1974 it provided training and work opportunities for black theatre artists. Unlike the N.E.C., it presented performances *in* the black community.

Following this lead, many black companies have emerged in major cities. Although their productions tend to be more traditional in form than those of some other minorities and the plays produced are not always by members of the company, they do provide an alternative to the more common theatre fare. They present productions from a black perspective that are by, for, and about black people.

Of equal importance are the Chicano theatres which began to form in the Southwestern United States in 1965. The first of these is the prototypical El Teatro Campesino (The Farmworkers Theatre). The Chicanos, of mixed American Indian and Spanish ancestry, have social handicaps not shared by blacks – for many Spanish is their first and sometimes their only language, which puts them at a scholastic and employment disadvantage. The productions usually make use of Mexican-style music and, so that they can be understood by everyone, are a bilingual mixture of Spanish and English. Only a few of the companies are sufficiently subsidized that their members can devote themselves full time to the theatre. Among these are El Teatro de la Gente (The Theatre of the People), formed in 1970 in San Jose, California, under the direction of Manuel Martinez and Adrian Vargas, who subsequently were instrumental in forming other Chicano theatres at the various colleges where they taught or offered workshops. El Teatro de la Esperanza (The Theatre of Hope) was founded in Santa Barbara, California, under the direction of Jorge Huerta in 1971. These groups perform primarily in Chicano communities – in cultural centres, churches, schools and parks. While they intend their productions primarily for other Chicanos, to raise their understanding of social and economic problems, their causes and solutions, the general population has shown increasing interest.

In the 1960s, as *laissez-faire* attitudes concerning life-style became more common, some homosexuals no longer hid their sexual orientation and a few overtly gay theatre groups were formed. As with other minority theatres, these groups helped to develop self-acceptance of their minority status and attempted to make themselves more acceptable to the community at large. Attempts by gay theatre groups to change social attitudes have taken two theatrical forms. Transvestite performances create sex-role confusion and ridicule strict social attitudes toward sex roles. This reduces the emphasis on sexual distinctions and orientation and focuses on individualism. Other groups present plays about the problems of homosexuals living in a predominantly heterosexual society.

The Play-House of the Ridiculous, formed in New York in 1965 by

20. *Bluebeard*

director–performer John Vaccaro and playwright Ronald Tavel, was the first of those groups employing transvestite performance. While the loose plots resemble camp parodies of old movies, the frenetic action involves a variety of sexual and scatological elements and reduces politics, society, religion, and sex to absurdity. In *Indira Gandhi's Daring Device* (1966) many sex acts were performed, including the use of a large dildo on Indira, while the characters talked of overpopulation and starvation.

In 1967 Charles Ludlam, an actor in Vaccaro's group, left and formed the Ridiculous Theatrical Company. Ludlam's company also uses cross-gender role creation. In *Bluebeard* (1970), based largely on a 1935 horror movie, Ludlam plays a sex-crazed doctor who is trying to develop a third sex and needs wives for experimentation. In his adaptation of *Camille* (1973) he plays the title role in an elaborate costume with his hairy chest showing,

21. *Razzmatazz*

vascillating between convincingly playing a woman and reminding the audience that he is a man. Ludlam believes that the audience comes to 'believe in the character beyond the gender of the actor, and no one who has experienced that can go back . . . It allows audiences to experience the universality of emotion, rather than believe that women are one species and men another.'[1]

The most exuberant gay group were the Cockettes, who came into being in San Francisco to celebrate New Year's Eve 1969. Previously, as members of a gay hippie commune, they had presented free spontaneous performances in the parks. Under the leadership of a man named Hibiscus, the Cockettes became a group of about twenty gays, straights, and young women who created productions in the style of camp Hollywood musicals of the 1940s. Their performances, intended primarily for the gay community of San Francisco, were anarchic and aggressively amateurish as they celebrated fun, dress-up, drag, exhibitionism, and sexual freedom. Soon Hibiscus left the group and formed the Angels of Light who gave their first performance on Christmas Eve 1970 at Grace Cathedral – a mock nativity scene in which Mary was played by a man in drag. Although the Cockettes disbanded soon afterwards, the San Francisco Angels of Light continued even after Hibiscus and his lover Angel Jack moved to New York and formed another company

22.   *Holy Cow*

of the same name. They continued the Cockettes tradition of living out show business fantasies in amateurish performances. In *Razzmatazz* (1974), a collection of production numbers and songs hang on a flimsy plot, singers miss notes, choreography is forgotten, headdresses fall off, and backstage whispers are heard. The company has child-like fun playing at being performers. The same unpretentiousness is present in the performances of the San Francisco group, but more attention is given to developing skill and polish. *Holy Cow* (1979) is a romantic story of long-ago and far-away India where a girl is forced to give up her lover and marry a tyrannical maharajah. However, the plot mainly serves as a structure for camp Indian palace drops, costumes, dances, acrobatics, and music. As always, men and women performers dress as either sex.

In the 1970s many gays and feminists came to consider transvestite performances offensive. They were seen as mocking women and misrepresenting gays. They did not deal with the problems of homosexuals. New companies were formed to deal seriously and realistically with the social issues. The Gay Theatre Collective, which began in San Francisco in 1976, was formed initially as a gay men's theatre and subsequently included lesbians. They create their productions collectively using improvisation, storytelling, discussion and writing, and present them to predominantly gay audiences.

In contrast with the gay theatre companies, those theatres which grew out of the women's movement are nearly always composed exclusively of women. The first objective of these theatres is expressed in the name of one of the earliest – the It's Alright to Be Woman Theatre formed in New York in 1970.

Roberta Sklar, who had co-directed some of the Open Theatre productions and worked with various women's groups, came to focus on presenting
a feminist analysis of human behaviour and a model for change. In 1976 she
began a collaboration with Clare Coss and Sondra Segal which became the
Women's Experimental Theatre. Their play, *The Daughter's Cycle Trilogy*,
is an exploration of women in the patriarchal family – the relationships of
mother–daughter and sister–sister – and an historical investigation of
violence toward women.

The theme of violence in relation to women has been the single most
important subject of women's plays in the second half of the seventies. The
multi-racial Spiderwoman Theatre Workshop collectively created *Women
in Violence* (1975) to offer 'support for women involved in the struggle
against violence and present alternatives to those who find themselves
trapped by "feminine" behaviour'. In the production the women tell their
own stories of violence interspersed with grotesque jokes of violence and
pornography told in a slap-stick style. Los Angeles visual artist Suzanne
Lacy has also dealt with this problem. *In Mourning and in Rage* (1977) presented a funeral procession of two-metre-tall figures dressed in black who
circled city hall memorializing the women who had been killed by the
'Hillside Strangler'.

The productions of Lilith – A Women's Theatre, formed in San Francisco
in 1975, have focused upon various concerns of women in society. Developing their work through improvisation, storytelling and writing, they attempt
'to expand the general public's understanding of women's lives'. Their first
play dealt with the personal concerns of women – menstruation, birth
control, lesbianism, mothers, masturbation, and celibacy. *Good Food* is the
story of five waitresses who learn to work together. *Moonlighting* is a play
about women and work based on the personal experiences of the company.
And *Pizza*, the first play to be written entirely by a single member of the
company, focuses upon the playwright's relationship to her mother and is set
in the family pizzeria. Through these plays the members of the company
have not only aimed at raising the consciousness of the general public to the
plight of women, but they have done what they would like society to do –
provide more theatre jobs for women.

Other people suffering discrimination by society have used theatre as a
means of articulating their needs, raising the awareness of fellow sufferers
and the public at large and, they hope, developing social and self-acceptance.
The National Theatre of the Deaf was formed in 1967 to provide opportunities for deaf actors. Their performances combine sign-language, mime,
dance, music, and narration to make their work accessible to all audiences.
The Family was formed in New York in 1972 to facilitate the re-entry of
ex-prisoners into society by providing opportunities for involvement in
theatre. They offer workshops and performances in prisons and elsewhere.
In San Francisco, Tale Spinners was formed in 1975 to provide performing
opportunities for elderly people and to create productions from the perspec-

tive of the aged. The Asian-American Theatre Workshop in San Francisco serves a similar function for their constituency.

Some of these companies believe, as does Joan Holden of the San Francisco Mime Troupe, that people will be moved to change society only when they know what they want. She calls upon the arts to 'piece together a vision of a better life so strong that people will finally insist on realizing it'.[2] Of course the 'vision of a better life' can be incorporated into the action of the play as an alternative to the existing society. But there are two other ways of demonstrating the better life – in the circumstances or spirit of the performance and its relationship to the audience, and in the collective organization of the group itself as a model for the improved society.

Companies such as the San Francisco Mime Troupe believe the theatre collective presents a model for a better society through the example of its own working conditions. There is no institutionalized hierarchy. Important decisions are made by the group, work and money are evenly distributed, and unpleasant tasks are shared. Group members focus on the co-operative making of a useful work rather than on individual self-expression. Director Luis Valdez says that the 'major emphasis' in the work of El Teatro Campesino 'is the social vision, as opposed to the individual artist or playwright's vision'.

Usually these theatres intend their plays for a specific constituency of people like themselves – blacks, Chicanos, gays, etc. – but they also want to perform for others. Not only is a larger audience important to their financial survival, but they also hope to reach outsiders who will come to understand their problems. Often those for whom the company particularly wants to perform, whether they be minorities or working people, do not usually attend the theatre. This has influenced their work in several ways.

The admission charge is usually low or spectators are encouraged to contribute what they can. Many groups go to the audience because they cannot expect the audience to come to them. Lilith has performed in women's prisons and in community centres. They provide free childcare at the performance. In the early days El Teatro Campesino performed at union meetings and labour camps. The San Francisco Mime Troupe performs each summer in the parks.

In order to attract and keep this atypical audience, they present work which is not identified with the established theatre, which the spectators have avoided or from which they have been excluded for financial or geographical reasons. One solution is the adaptation of popular entertainment techniques. This is not a condescension, but a recognition of the entertainment values of such techniques and their appeal to the public at large. They have borrowed techniques from *commedia dell'arte,* as is evident in the stereotypes, masks, and broad comic action of El Teatro Campesino. The Pickle Family Circus in San Francisco incorporates circus techniques into their performances. The San Francisco Mime Troupe has a band and for a time they began their performances with juggling exhibitions. Popular entertainment techniques are not only fun, but in them the performers do not hide themselves completely in their characters and, therefore, they can relate to the spectators as real persons. It is important for the *performer* to be present – not merely the fictional character.

Some of these companies are content to change the attitudes of those present. Others, however, would rally those present into a force which can have an effect upon society at large. In either case it is important that the performance create a community among the spectators and between the spectators and the performers. For this to happen the spectator must be psychically present in actual time so as to acknowledge other spectators with like interests and concerns. In the traditional theatre the spectator is a recipient – sitting in the dark relating privately to the work. If it is successful, it empties the spectator's mind of the actual present because he focuses upon the fictional illusions. The artists take care that the play does not direct the focus to events in the real world because it would distract the spectator from the fictional world. In the traditional theatre only fictional time is important. In the theatre of social purpose actual time and real events are important. If the spectator's focus becomes wholly absorbed in the illusion, it must periodically be brought back to the actual world. The spectator must be psychically present in order to form a community with others and to make the necessary connection between the events in the play, the conditions referred to, and the circumstances of her or her own life.

Aside from the use of popular entertainment techniques, the most universally practised means for distancing the illusion and creating a relationship between the performer and spectator is a kind of acting similar to that described by Brecht. The performer *demonstrates* the character rather than *becoming* the character. Instead of becoming submerged in the fiction to the extent of being indistinguishable from the character, the performer is seen through the character as is the person who tells a story and enacts some of the people in it. Charles Ludlam of the Ridiculous Theatrical Company says the performer should seem to be winking at the audience. In most transvestite performances the spectator sees simultaneously (or at least alternatingly) the performer of one sex and the character of the other. Another technique is for the performers to talk informally with the audience before the performance. The Provisional Theatre's production of *Xa: A Vietnam Primer* begins with each of the performers talking to a small group of spectators, encouraging them to ask questions about the large map of Vietnam outlined on the acting area. Members of the San Francisco Mime Troupe always mingle with the audience before the performance and during performance they break the illusion by commenting on unplanned events as when a dog wanders on stage. Many groups hold discussions with their audiences after performances. This demystifies the performers so they can be seen as people sharing the same concerns as their audience, and it reinforces the concept of characters as illusions created by the performers for the purpose of demonstration. Such discussions also assist the spectator in relating the stage events to the realities of society.

Some groups invent ways for the spectators to be physically active in contrast with their traditionally passive role. By moving from place to place during a performance, the spectator not only breaks the illusion of the fictional world but changes the viewing perspective and thereby exercises a prerogative that does not exist for the audience of television, cinema, or traditional theatre.

The interaction of performers and spectators helps create a sense of community which on some occasions results in an exuberant communal expression at the end of a performance, as when spectators danced with performers at the conclusion of a performance by El Teatro Campesino at the Mexican pyramids of Teotihuacan. At least temporarily a small change takes place in the society that is present. A single performance may not have a great impact upon the society at large, but these companies believe that each performance potentially brings society closer to the better world the theatre groups envisage. Most such groups see themselves as part of a larger movement which can bring about significant social change.

Those contemporary theatre groups who intend a social efficacy have developed a mode of theatre that is distinct from the traditional twentieth-century theatre. In the creation of a community such theatre resembles that of certain periods before the advent of naturalism, and it is the closest twentieth-century theatre has come to the communal festivals in ancient Greece where Western theatre originated.

The San Francisco Mime Troupe

The San Francisco Mime Troupe gave its first performances in 1959, making it one of the oldest of the contemporary theatres dedicated to bringing about social change. Although at the outset the founder of the theatre, R.G. Davis, did not speak of political intentions or of a desire to perform for a non-traditional audience, these objectives were implicit in the direction he gave the theatre from the very beginning. Throughout its history the San Francisco Mime Troupe has focused on forms of entertainment which historically have appealed to people regardless of their social, economic, or educational status and has avoided those forms which tend to be more contemplative than energetic. In keeping with other political theatres of the last twenty years they have used techniques from *commedia dell'arte,* circus, puppet shows, music hall, vaudeville, parades, magicians, carnival side shows, buskers, brass bands, comic strips, melodrama, minstrel shows, and other means of exhilarating entertainment.

R.G. Davis set out to explore a theatrical form which was in clear contrast to the psychological realism of the established theatres. His company performed silent mime in the common man tradition of Charlie Chaplin and Buster Keaton – not that of the more aesthete Marcel Marceau. They focused on the use of body movement to convey action, character, and attitude, thus already forming the basis for a unique style. Soon they added words to their performances and their historical model became *commedia dell'arte*.

In 1962 the Mime Troupe took a major step toward broadening their audience. They began performing in the parks of San Francisco and made an effort to attract neighbourhood people to their shows. While the early indoor audience had been predominantly young middle-class intellectuals, the audience in the parks varied, depending on the neighbourhood. In the North Beach area there were beatniks and hippies, but the Mime Troupe also got the interest of the working people in the area, who were mainly of Italian and Chinese extraction. In the Mission district the neighbourhood consisted of working people, but their core audience of young intellectuals followed them wherever they played. It was a difficult transition to the open air because there was no tradition for performances in the parks and because the plays being performed were far from innocuous in their language and politics. The resulting struggle with the authorities brought them the support of the young New Left. In 1965 Davis was arrested when the group performed after a permit had been denied on the basis that there was 'vulgar' material in the script. The action was appealed and the denial was ruled an unconstitutional attempt at censorship. Since then the Mime Troupe has spent the summer of each year giving free performances on a portable stage in the parks of San Francisco.

From 1962 until 1970 the staple of the group was adaptations of scripts by Molière, Goldoni, Machiavelli, Beolco, Bruno, and Lope de Rueda, performed in the manner of *commedia dell'arte* with the traditional stereotype masked characters, exaggerated movement and voice, and sufficient flexibility to incorporate news event of the day and to permit impromptu responses to unplanned events during the performance. The *commedia* style served well to hold attention and compete with the usual outdoor distractions. Each of these adaptations, while keeping the traditional characters and costuming, was infused with the general political radicalism of the San Francisco hip scene of the mid-1960s.

An adaptation of Goldoni's *L'Amant militaire* in 1967 became their first long anti-Vietnam play. The plot is mostly from Goldoni. The Spanish army is fighting in Italy, a clear parallel with the U.S. army in Vietnam. Pantalone, the mayor, connives with the Spanish general to profit from the war. The general is determined 'to pursue peace with every available weapon'. Pantalone would marry his daughter off to the old general, but she is secretly in love with a young lieutenant. Arlecchino disguises himself as a woman in order to avoid military service. In the end, the soubrette, dressed like the Pope, appears above the curtain and stops the war. She then tells the audience: 'If you want something done my friends – do it yourselves.'

The *commedia* stereotypes of authoritarian well-to-do old man, general, young lovers, soubrette and tricky servant, had undergone some changes, but in appearance were still very much traditional *commedia* with half masks

23. *L'Amant militaire,* **photo: San Francisco Mime Troupe**

and costumes. Further, the names were unchanged and the plots, while somewhat adapted, were still more from an Italian past than an American present.

In 1969 the group began experimenting with different styles. They spent many months working on a production of Brecht's last unfinished play, *The Congress of the White Washers*, a clearly Marxist play produced in the style of a Chinese opera. The conflicts brought into the open by their work on the play resulted in a series of meetings held to resolve differences respecting the focus and the organization of the company. The discussions are recalled by Joan Holden who has become the principle playwright of the group.[3]

The company was divided ideologically. The conscious Marxists believed that they should focus on playing for the working class. Davis, however, was convinced that they should aim their work at pre-revolutionary young

61

middle-class intellectuals. Furthermore, some were determined that the Mime Troupe become a collective in its structure with all decisions made by the group as a whole. Davis, however, was equally determined that he continue as the company's sole director and make all important decisions himself. The conflicts culminated in Davis and the most militant of the Marxists leaving the company. Those who remained felt leaderless. Partly for this reason and partly on principle they formed a theatre collective. The structure of the organization came to reflect the ideals presented in their plays as they made the shift from intellectuals commenting on political issues to political activists; from artists who had a proprietary attitude about their individual contributions to art workers with a common objective of bringing about social change.

Since 1970 each of the Mime Troupe's productions has focused upon a political problem selected by the group. Most often the plays have been written by Joan Holden, sometimes in collaboration with other company members, but the programmes have rarely carried the name of any individual as they have preferred to take collective credit for their productions. Despite scripting by individuals, the plays express the consensus of the group as developed through study and discussion of the political issue by the entire company.

The first production after reorganization as a collective was also the first of their productions to break with the *commedia* style. Joan Holden recalls that while they liked *commedia* because the characters were clear, it had a broad comic style, and it was funny, they were dissatisfied with it because it was foreign. They had been searching for an American equivalent, and they found it in a parody of nineteenth-century melodrama. *The Independent Female, or A Man Has His Pride!* (1970) was written by Holden in this style. American stereotypes of the capitalist, the young naive man and the strong woman were used in much the same way as the *commedia* stereotypes.

This women's liberation play, set in the nineteenth century, concerns Gloria Pennybank who is engaged to marry a junior executive, John Heartright. Gloria, however, is unhappy because, although she likes her job, John insists that when they are married she must quit. He wants 'a wife, not a business partner'. The villain is Sarah Bullitt, a feminist who persuades Gloria that 'femininity is a drug to make us slave'. Together they lead a women's strike for equal pay, free nurseries, and free transportation. To frustrate Gloria's leadership, John resorts to deception. He holds a gun to his head and threatens to kill himself if Gloria does not sign an agreement to renounce all of her political activities and live for him alone. She relents and is about to sign when Sarah pulls a gun on John and exposes his deceit. John takes advantage of the confusion and shoots Sarah who dies. After all, she is the villain. Gloria renounces her love forever and vows to work for the cause.

The original version of the play had followed the melodrama form more closely, but it was strongly criticized by a group of feminists who suggested

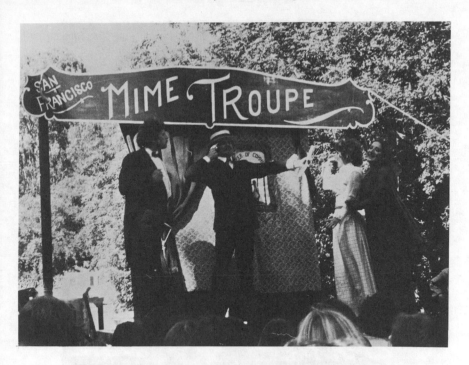

24. *The Independent Female or A Man Has His Pride!*

changes. In the earlier version Sarah's ironic villainy was maintained more strictly so that she was a manipulative woman who cast a spell on innocent Gloria in order to destroy all men. The first version of the play was also criticized for its mock happy ending in which Gloria gave up her fight and returned to John. During the course of the discussions with the feminists the Mime Troupe decided it was important to resolve the conflict between the form and the message on the side of their political intent.

Another potential danger in *The Independent Female* was that some spectators might not distinguish between the parody of the melodrama form and the seriousness of the political statement and take the play as a spoof of the women's liberation movement. In the next major play this problem was averted. Its form was not specifically from the past, but borrowed elements from the old melodrama, from *commedia,* from the spy movie, and even from comic strips. In part, this diffuse form may have come about because the scenario of *The Dragon Lady's Revenge* (1971) was developed collectively by five members through discussion, and then each wrote assigned scenes.

The Dragon Lady's Revenge was set in the present (1971) in the 'capital of Cochin, a small country in S.E. Asia'. A young American lieutenant, the son of the U.S. Ambassador, attempts to find the man who murdered his friend with an overdose of heroin. He becomes a pawn in the power struggle

25. *The Dragon Lady's Revenge*

between those running the drug traffic – the Dragon Lady, General Rong Q who is head of the country, and the C.I.A. In the end they are exposed by Blossom, a member of the N.L.F. who works as a B-girl in the den of iniquity run by the Dragon Lady. When Mr Big, the man behind the drug traffic, is revealed to be the American Ambassador, his son changes sides and joins Blossom.

The stereotypes are mostly a blend from forms previously used by the Mime Troupe. The lieutenant and Blossom are the young lovers from *commedia* or melodrama. The U.S. Ambassador is a blend of Pantalone and the capitalist boss of *The Independent Female*. General Rong Q is a cross between the Capitano of *commedia* and the intriguing villain of foreign espionage movies. An agent of the Ambassador who makes each appearance in a different disguise is like one of the *commedia zanni*. The Dragon Lady is the evil woman of von Sternberg films and the comic strip *Terry and the Pirates*.

26. *The Dragon Lady's Revenge*

While masks were not used in *The Independent Female* or *The Dragon Lady's Revenge,* the acting style was broad enough to accommodate a man playing the mother and a woman General Rong Q. Both pieces used devices such as overhead conversations, disguises, mock heroic speeches, slapstick comedy, surprise revelations, and endings that provided models for action by the spectators.

Although the Mime Troupe had come to think of themselves as art *workers,* the subjects of their plays continued to come more from the intellectual Left than from the working class. No doubt this resulted in part from the fact that their core audience continued to be made up of this group and in part because most members came from middle-class backgrounds or had recently been students. Furthermore, it was not altogether clear who constituted the working class. In practical terms, according to Joan Holden, the Mime Troupe came to think of working people as those who are difficult to reach. They are the people who work for wages, who are not college educated, and who think the theatre is not for them – people who watch television and attend sports events but think that theatre is for an educated elite. Since 1971 most of the productions of the Mime Troupe have been concerned with the issues of working people in an attempt to serve this audience.

For several years in the early 1970s the group began performances with an exhibition of juggling, a skill developed by most members of the company.

27. *Frozen Wages*

In *Frozen Wages* (1972), a protest against Nixon's price and wage control policies, juggling was integrated into the action of the play to represent an assembly line. At first six workers juggle six clubs, leisurely tossing them to one another. Then, a figure resembling the State of Liberty suggests to the Boss that while price controls prohibit him from raising prices, he can increase profits by reducing expenses. How? By firing some of his workers. One-by-one he fires workers until only two are left to juggle all of the clubs. The Boss is still not satisfied with his profits, so, at the suggestion of the government representative, he steps up production – faster and faster until one of the worker–jugglers becomes catatonic. Eventually, a strike provides a solution for the workers who force the Boss to accept more humane working conditions.

About this time the Mime Troupe was attempting to resolve an issue concerning the composition of the company. In 1971, when they would go each Friday noon to the docks to play music and juggle for the longshoremen ,on strike, the question of race arose. The performers were all white. The longshoremen were mostly black. In fact, the working people in San Francisco were largely non-white. The Mime Troupe knew they must become multi-racial. Their affirmative action programme got underway in 1974 and by 1980 the membership of the company was seven white, five Latin, and three black. They were able to play for a black church in Illinois, a Mexican farm workers' picnic in Texas, a Filipino organization in Oakland, the Californian prison system, and anybody in San Francisco.

The Great Air Robbery (1974) had a black hero even though it did not focus on a specifically working-class issue. In this parody of a television detective story, Ray Von is hired by Hugh G. Magnum, an oil capitalist, to protect one of his inventors, Violet Mince. When Ray Von goes to her house and discovers her dead, he vows to find her killer. Meanwhile, because of increasing air pollution, it has become difficult to breathe. The capitalist is making another fortune by selling air, but only to those who can pay and are not 'trouble makers'. Ray Von finally figures out that Violet Mince was killed because she had invented a way of converting sunshine to energy by using plants, and this solar energy would ruin Hugh G. Magnum's plans to control the world. Ray Von finds the hidden plays and gives them to the Red Bat, a people's revolutionary group which is the only hope of the world.

The relationship between those who grow the food and those who control its distribution is explored in *Frijoles or Beans* (1975). *('Frijoles'* is the Spanish word for 'beans'.) Two couples, a poor man and wife who grow bananas in a South American country and a poor unemployed man and wife in the United States, discover that they have much in common – hunger and unsatisfying lives. The U.S. housewife finds a note put in her banana by the woman who grew it which says 'Somebody gets ripped off, you know, when somebody else gets rich. Ask who wants things this way?' When they ask, they see the answer – international capitalists, those who own the food, the land, the stores, and the government. The two couples find that they have a common enemy, and through a series of comic reversals force the U.S. Secretary of Agriculture and Henry Kissinger, who represent all the evil forces, to feed the world, to stay out of Third World countries, and to stop manipulating world affairs.

In 1976, to commemorate the American bicentennial year, the Mime Troupe presented the longest and most complex play written within the group. *False Promises/Nos Engañaron* (Spanish meaning 'We've been had') is a two-hour play with songs which places the events of American history into a materialist context. Again the central characters are working people – in this instance miners. It is their first play to borrow from the style of the American western movie, but it owes more to Brecht than to John Wayne. The company's intent is serious analysis, but the play is entertaining because of skilful acting, dancing, and songs, and because the play connects the historical events with the emotions of working-class characters involved in everyday activities.

The play concerns the year 1898–9 when the United States formulated overseas expansionist policies which took American military forces to Cuba, Puerto Rico, and the Philippines in what is known as the Spanish–American War. The effect of this policy is shown through three carefully interrelated stories which provide three perspectives. It is seen from the top in Washington, D.C., where plans are made to extend the country's economic influence

28. *False Promises/Nos Engañaron*

to create new markets for American capitalism. The effects of the policy are
experienced from the bottom by the citizens of a Colorado town where
copper, an essential war material, is being mined. The impact of the policy is
also felt by a black soldier who is sent to suppress black people in Puerto
Rico. The three stories collide at the end of the play.

The Prologue is set in a polling place in South Carolina on election day
1896, the day on which William McKinley was elected President of the
United States. Washington Jefferson, a black man, attempts to vote. A
lynch mob is formed, but he escapes. The scene shifts to the White House in
the spring of 1898. The king of high finance, J.P. Morgan, persuades President McKinley to extend the country's economic influence and create new
markets for American capitalism. Colonel Theodore Roosevelt has the solution. 'Our destiny's manifest: to liberate Spain's island colonies, and then to
keep them.'

The next scene focuses on the central story. In a small town in Colorado,
copper miners want to strike for the eight-hour workday, but whites and
Mexicans are divided. The news arrives that the battleship Maine has been
blown up at Havana, signalling the start of war with Spain. Casey, a socialist
miner, opposes the conflict as a bosses' war; Charlie, the union chieftain,
who sees a strike as threatening to his power, argues that the war boom will
improve wages and conditions without a sturggle. The pivotal character,

29. *False Promises*

Harry (brave but ignorant, he is the Troupe's stock character of the white American worker), sees no contradiction between the war and the strike. 'Hell, we'll take the Spaniards on with one hand, and the mine owners with the other!' His confusion is amusing, but the miners' failure to see that imperialism is good for the owners, not the workers, contributes to the eventual failure of the strike.

The tragic death of a Mexican miner brings about an uneasy alliance between whites and Mexicans; but even as they shake hands, Casey admits to the Mexican leaders that racism will not disappear overnight: 'Us whites have been hating for a long time. We had to, to take over this country.'

The theme of racism permeates the play, and lends it much of its impact. Some members of this multi-racial company have described the rehearsals for *False Promises* as 'racial encounter therapy'. The play, however, does not treat racism as a psychological problem, but as an historical one. It is an instance of what is seen as people's deepest failing: the blindness to their true self-interest which leads them to fight others of their class instead of joining them. In different ways, all the working-class characters (except the socialist) defeat themselves by fighting for 'me and mine' against people who should be their allies. Washington Jefferson joins the army to win advancement for black Americans, and finds himself suppressing black Puerto Ricans; because the war is supposed to mean jobs at home, Harry's wife

30. *False Promises*

(Belle) sends her brother off to get killed; Harry betrays the Mexicans to save the white miners' jobs, and precipitates the disaster that engulfs everyone.

When Copper City is occupied by the same army that has fought the Filipinos, the townsfolk who have supported the war begin to understand that the promises of imperialism are false. There has been too much racism and betrayal to allow for a sentimental vision of unity, but the black soldier ends the play on a pragmatic note:

> When the time comes, you don't get to pick who's on your side – history decides that for you. You just got to understand history.

In form and style as well as in content *False Promises* represents a synthesis of several years work. Discussions which ultimately led to its making were begun in 1973 when the group considered the possibility of making a play on the history of the U.S. labour movement, but having insufficient time for such a large project they produced Brecht's *The Mother* instead. When discussions resumed in the summer of 1975 they set out to make a 'people's history' for the American bicentennial year. In January 1976, after an intervening tour, they began their research by reading materialist histories of the United States and inviting speakers from the labour movement – mainly from union 'radical caucuses' – to give political education sessions.

Copper City,
Colorado
March 1899

31. *False Promises*

The company divided up into smaller groups which met separately in order to develop possible scenario ideas. These scenarios were then presented to the entire company for discussion. Inevitably there were frictions as members became advocates for competing scenarios. After weeks of discussion, the scenario which had been put forward by Joan Holden prevailed and she was assigned to write the script. However, the play came from a collective concept developed and tested through months of reading, discussion, and rehearsals in which members of the company continued to participate in the development of the play as questions arose and were resolved.

False Promises is stylistically the most complex of the Mime Troupe's plays. Holden adapted Shakespeare's device of a main plot presenting heroic figures speaking in blank verse and a sub-plot of low characters speaking in prose. But the 'heroic' figures are the comic ones, and the 'low' characters are taken seriously. They had learned with Brecht's *The Mother* that a style of heightened realism could be made to work outdoors, so they could abandon older styles which they now found too limiting. So the working-class characters in the new play, although based on comic types, were made realistically complex. They are sympathetic, but are not drawn as simplistically good.

The style, however, is quite different from that of illusionistic realism. In part this is because of the need to heighten and energize the acting to make it carry outdoors, as well as the necessity of dealing with distractions such as a drunk coming onto the stage. But in addition the style of acting, derived from mime, results in gestures which not only express the character but are also the actor's comment on the character. The audience, because it is not completely absorbed into the fictional illusion, is able to see the ideas in relation to the real world, and that is of course the major focus of the Mime Troupe's work.

The energetic heightened realism of *False Promises* became the style of two subsequent plays which focus on working-class issues. *Hotel Universe* (1977) by Joan Holden returns to the issue of urban renewal dealt with in *High Rises* and *San Fran Scandals of '73*. The events of the play loosely parallel the actual events at San Francisco's International Hotel. The eccentric elderly tenants of Hotel Universe are threatened with eviction by a real-estate speculator who wants to demolish the hotel so as to use the property in a more lucrative way. The down-and-nearly-out inhabitants include a long-shoreman who has been replaced by a machine, a former hot dog vendor named Gladys, the lady who used to run the bumper cars at Playland, and a retired prima ballerina. This multi-racial group, instead of being intimidated by the march of capitalism, unites the working community in opposition. Although they eventually lose their battle, as did the tenants of the International Hotel, they see their fight as a model for those who follow. While the characters are realistic, the show includes band music, songs, comic pantomime, and energy that is exuberant beyond reality.

Electro-Bucks (1978), by Holden and Peter Solomon, is set in an electronics factory in 'Silicon Valley' (the Santa Clara Valley just south of San Francisco) which, typical of the industry, employs mostly minority women at low wages. The female workers in the play are supervised by Henderson, the production manager of the factory who was born Hernandez but thinks the anglo image will help him advance faster. He is attracted to Dela, a new Chicana worker, but comically tries to resist the temptation and maintain his new identity. When business exigencies result in the firing of Edith, Dela uses Henderson's love to save her colleague's job and put the workers in charge of the factory.

While the company has managed to work full time at theatre for many years, their economic conditions are difficult. The donations the company receives from passing the hat in the parks do not pay their salaries and other expenses even for the summer. During the autumn and spring they usually tour to other parts of the country and to Europe. In 1980 they became the first American theatre to tour Cuba since the revolution. Although their work is well received – they have been awarded Obies for at least two of their productions – financially they barely survive.

The Troupe has played two Decembers in a row at the Victoria Theatre, an ex-burlesque house in San Francisco's Mission District, and is encouraged by the broad audience it draws there. Says Joan Holden, 'I dream of the Victoria in a few years as a mini-version of the French T.N.P. [Théâtre national populaire] – packed out with subscriptions sold through union

32. *Electro-Bucks*

caucuses and grass-roots organizations.'

Despite more than twenty years of financial poverty, the San Francisco Mime Troupe has continued its commitment to audiences who normally are culturally disenfranchised. While such audiences are probably the least lucrative, they are essential to the company's objective of bringing about social change. Joan Holden points out that change will not come from people who are comfortable in the system, it will come from those who are made uncomfortable by it. 'The basic theme of all our plays is the same: there is a class system in this country that is not run in your interest. It is run in the interest of rich people and they fool you about your interest.'

It is the objective of the Mime Troupe to help those who do not benefit from the system to understand what is in their self-interest and to see that change is possible. But this can only be accomplished, according to Joan Holden, by breaking down the atomization of working-class life.

> Television has tended to put an end to bars, theatres, and social clubs. It keeps people isolated in their homes, keeps their focus on personal problems and private issues to the exclusion of public or community issues. This is a massive weight holding people down and keeping them from bringing about change.

It is this weight that the Mime Troupe is trying to lift. It is Holden's conviction that theatre can function as a shared communal event much as it did in primitive societies and in ancient Greece. The Mime Troupe wants to make that experience available to people who have been deprived of a community life, in order to restore that life in some small degree. There is a sense of community from gathering together to share a common experience, and that sense of community is important because people know they cannot change the world by themselves. The potential for change is felt when they are part of an energy, a movement, that is bigger than they are.

> When we do the right show at the right time for the right people on the right subject, the energy that surges up from the audience gives a taste of what people really moving could be like.

El Teatro Campesino
(The Farmworkers Theatre)

In 1965 Luis Valdez, then a theatre student in California, saw a *commedia* performance by the San Francisco Mime Troupe. He was so amazed by the vitality, the colour and the sound that he joined the troupe. At about the same time he began thinking of a theatre for farmworkers which would bring together his roots as the son of migrant labourers and his theatre training. He was convinced that if any theatre would appeal to farmworkers it would be the lively, bawdy, outdoor style of the Mime Troupe.

It was also in 1965 that the National Farm Workers Association of Cesar Chavez, after three years of development, first began to test its strength by joining the Agricultural Workers Organizing Committee in a strike against the grape growers in Delano, California, Valdez says that he knew he had to do something, so he talked to officers of the union about the value of the farmworkers' theatre. They were encouraging, so he decided to go to Delano, where he was born in 1940, and attempt to start a theatre.

Nearly all of the field workers were Chicanos – that is, of American Indian and Spanish ancestry – which made organizing very difficult. The only work available to most of them was in the fields, as they had poor or non-existent formal education and limited English. Typically they considered themselves fortunate to have a job, so they were reluctant to strike even though their low wages kept them at poverty level. Progress toward forming a viable union was slow. The situation was further aggravated by Mexican workers who illegally slipped across the border, often with the help of labour contractors, and were willing to work as scabs for whatever payment they were offered. They could make no demands without the threat of deportation.

The strike had been in effect for a month when Valdez arrived in Delano and met one evening in the house behind the union office with a group of union volunteers. These workers and students spent their days attempting to persuade those who were still picking grapes to join the strike. Valdez had brought some signs along made for the occasion. He hung signs saying

Huelgista (striker) on two of the men and *Esquirol* (scab) on a third who was instructed to act like a scab. The *Huelgistas* started shouting at the scab and everyone began laughing.[4] It was the beginning of El Teatro Campesino.

For about three weeks the small group spent their days on the picket line, and at night they worked on skits. Then they gave their first presentation in Filipino Hall. Soon a pattern was established. The company would spend most of their time in the cities performing to raise money for the strike and return to Delano to provide entertainment for weekly union meetings. During the 1966 historic 300-mile 25-day march to Sacramento which brought press attention to the union, the Teatro provided entertainment at each night's rally. In preparation for the election which would resolve the jurisdictional dispute between the Farm Workers Union and the Teamsters Union, the group was sent to the labour camps to perform and organize.

The theatrical form which had taken shape came to be called the *acto*. It was a short bilingual skit of perhaps fifteen minutes dealing in a comic way with situations in the lives of Chicano workers. They were short enough for use on a picket line, and three or four could be put together for a longer programme. The style of performance was similar to that of the San Francisco Mime Troupe as adapted from *commedia dell'arte*. Taking the Mexican mime Cantinflas as their model, they used broad energetic movement that could convey a situation even without words, and some performers wore masks which highlighted the stereotype characters. Because the audience consisted of monolingual Spanish and English speakers as well as those who were bilingual, the Teatro's plays were always a mixture of two languages – a practice which is common in the everyday language of the *barrios*.

Each *acto* made a specific point. In *Las Dos Caras del Patroncito (The Two Faces of the Boss)*, first performed in 1965 on the picket line, the scab is shown as the second face of the Boss. The Boss, wearing a pig-like mask, attempts to persuade one of his scab farmworkers that it is better to be a worker than to have the burdensome responsibilities of a boss. He is so persuasive that he convinces himself, and the Farmworker and Boss exchange roles. The Boss discovers his mistake, but the Farmworker refuses to trade back. The performance ends with the Boss calling for the help of Cesar Chavez and shouting '*Huelga!*'

Valdez was finding it difficult to direct a theatre company that was a part of the union. The performers' primary obligation was to the union and the strike needed everyone to help with such activities as organizing a grape boycott. The quality of the theatre suffered and it was difficult to make plans. However, they managed their first national tour in the summer of 1967 to raise funds and publicize the strike. But when they returned, El Teatro Campesino became independent of the union and moved to Del Rey, a small suburb of Fresno about sixty miles north of Delano.

In their new location the group established El Centro Campesino Cultural (The Farmworkers Cultural Center) and their objectives expanded. As in other minority movements, the Chicano movement (La Raza) was

33. *Las Dos Caras del Patroncito*

attempting to identify and emphasize its own unique cultural attributes. At the Center Valdez and his associates taught classes in music, history, drama, English, Spanish, and practical politics. While they continued to support the union and to perform the *huelga actos,* the subjects of their new plays broadened to include various aspects of Chicano life and concerns.

Los Vendidos (The Sellouts, 1967) was concerned with Chicano stereotypes and tokenism in government hiring. A secretary from Governor Reagan's office comes to Honest Sancho's Used Mexican Lot and Curio Shop to find 'a Mexican type for the administration'. She is shown several models. There is the Farmworker whom Sancho describes as the Volkswagen of Mexico, very economical, a few pennies a day keeps him going on tortillas and beans. The secretary is impressed by the economical advantages, but when she discovers that he doesn't speak English she moves on to

34. *Las Dos Caras del Patroncito*

Johnny Pachuco who runs on hamburgers, beer, and marijuana. Johnny has all of the necessities for city life – he dances, he fights with a knife, and he steals. Other models include the Revolucionario, a genuine antique, who has starred in all of the Pancho Villa movies and runs on raw horse meat and tequila. There is the Mexican-American who wears a business suit and tie. Sancho explains that he is just like the white model but he comes in several colours. He is a bit more expensive to run as he requires dry martinis. He eats Mexican food only on ceremonial occasions. The secretary thinks he is perfect and makes the purchase. However, as soon as money changes hands, the Mexican-American shouts, *'Viva la huelga',* and all of the models chase the secretary away and divide the money.

In 1969 the company moved to Fresno which had a metropolitan population of 300,000 including many Chicanos. In this urban environment they continued their objectives of education and agitation by presenting plays concerned with various aspects of Chicano culture. In *The Militants* (1969), a five-minute play, comes the first indication of the company's worries about the movement – the internal conflicts, the tendency of some Chicanos to engage in stirring rhetoric and rallies while leaving the boring and arduous door-to-door work to others. The play makes the point that the outward show of militancy can be assimilated by the system with no real changes resulting. A white professor greets the audience and explains how pleased he is to welcome a militant speaker who will 'tell it like it is' and 'sock it to us'. It turns out that two militant speakers claim to be the one invited, so they take turns speaking in increasingly violent rhetoric. While each begins by agreeing with the other, they soon find fault with what the other has said. The professor assents to each of the disparaging comments about him and the establishment of which he is a part. In the end the two militants shoot each other. The professor announces the conclusion of the lecture, and through his laughter says, 'I feel so guilty'.

It was not long before the conflicts within his own company and the movement as a whole caused Valdez to shift the focus and style of the Teatro. But in the meantime they continued to use the *acto* style to present plays dealing with a variety of social, economic, and political concerns in the Chicano community.

Vietnam Campesino (1970) is a particularly complex *acto* touching upon several issues: the need to protect farmworkers from pesticides sprayed in the fields, the disadvantage Chicanos faced with respect to the draft, the problems of maintaining an effective boycott against non-union grapes when the Defence Department was buying such grapes for the military, the importance of recognizing that Vietnamese peasants and Chicano farmworkers have a common enemy in the American military–agricultural–business establishment. The play draws parallels between the conditions of the farmworkers in the United States on one side of the stage and the peasants of Vietnam on the other.

In 1971 Teatro Campesino and its cultural centre moved to a new permanent home in San Juan Bautista, a small town which is the site of a Franciscan mission built at the end of the eighteenth century by Indians under the direction of Catholic priests from Spain. Such a move had become important because of the urban distractions of Fresno and frictions within the group. Shortly before this Valdez had commented that although sloganeering was a necessary part of any political movement he was beginning to hunger for something else – a 'greater spirituality'.[5] He had come to believe that the frictions among those in the company came from a misdirected anger. The more they 'called for a fighting spirit, the more that same spirit manifested itself in terms of internal conflict'. Hostility against an unjust system was vented on each other. It destroyed the unity that was needed to continue and was in opposition to the reasons for doing their work – the brotherhood of Chicanos.

35. *Vietnam Campesino*

While the company continued to support the union and to work for social change, they were searching for a deeper spirituality. Since the group consisted of Chicanos, who were part American Indian – Valdez is part Yaqui – it was natural that the search would lead them to Mayan philosophy and practices. The Mayas, whose culture dates back to about 2000 B.C., were the intellectuals of ancient America; they developed a glyph-writing and complex calendix and built in the jungles of Yucatan, Chiapas, Guatemala and Honduras monumental ceremonial centres which were the earthly seats of their theocracy. In San Juan Bautista the members of the Teatro formed a community based on the Mayan model. They bought two houses where they lived communally, and on forty acres of land adjacent to the town they farmed according to Mayan practices. Their social lives were influenced by Indian philosophy, especially the Indian version of the Golden Rule – 'You are my other self'.

Their theatre work was also influenced by their study of Indian philosophy and mythology. Like the Mayas, they came to believe that people must be in harmony with other human beings and with nature or violence will result. No longer was the aim of their theatre work to rally the Chicano community against those who were seen as oppressors, but to harmonize the individual with mankind and with the cosmos. They still believed in social causes, but according to Luis Valdez 'the greatest cause that unifies all mankind is the first cause, and that is god' – an expression of ultimate humanity whether symbolized by Jesus Christ, Quetzalcoatl, Mohammed, Buddha, or other god–men who have existed. Thus, according to Valdez, 'the cause of social justice becomes tied to the cause of everything else in our universe and in the cosmos'.

From the outset Valdez associated the realism of the dominant American theatre with the American 'hang-up on the material aspects of human existence'. In the published collection of Teatro Campesino *actos* (1971), he calls for a Chicano theatre that is 'revolutionary in technique as well as content' which would educate the people 'toward an appreciation of *social change'*.[6]

The *acto* had served the needs of the union and specific social issues, but the new interest of the company in their ancient American roots led to the development of a new form which they called the *mito* (myth). Almost from the beginning of El Teatro Campesino some characters in their plays were non-human. In 1965 actors played the title roles in *Three Grapes*. The following year, in *Quinta Temporada (Fifth Season),* the cast of characters included Winter, Spring, Summer, and Fall. And in *Vietnam Campesino,* El Draft, wearing a death mask, takes away the young Chicano farmworker. The company had also dressed as *calaveras* (skeletons) for various events, borrowing the image from Mexican folklore. The *mito,* however, went even further in its use of non-human characters.

In *Bernabe* (*c*. 1969) mythological figures are used in a central way. The title character, a village idiot in a Californian *campesino* town, is confronted by Luna (Moon) dressed as a 1940s *pachuco* who arranges an assignation with his beautiful sister Tierra (Earth). She tempts Bernabe into trying to seduce her, but is told she must ask her father El Sol (the sun) for permission to marry. El Sol appears as the Aztec Sun God and the play is resolved through the Aztec ritual of offering a human heart to the sun god so that he can continue to feed life. Bernabe is sacrificed and resurrected as a cosmic man. La Tierra is again pure.

The work which most directly reflected their Mayan interests in the early 1970s is *El Baile de los Gigantes (The Dance of the Giants,* 1974). It is their most mystical work, yet it is intended to have a social efficacy. The production is a re-creation of a ceremony that has been performed for at least a thousand years by the Chorti Indians of Yucatan. The Chorti ceremony, in turn, is based upon the mythology of the Mayan sacred book, the *Popul Vuh (People's Book),* an account of the cosmogony, mythology, traditions, and history of the Mayan people. It is presented at noon on the summer solstice and is intended to assure the well-being of the community.

The performance concerns the gods before the first dawn and tells how the sun and moon of our ancestors were created, thus preparing for the creation of man. It is narrated by Valdez and performed by eight dancers and musicians playing drum, cymbal, flute, rattles, guitar, and conch shell. Frequently the performers accompany their movement and singing. The movement, usually dance steps, is geometrical and precisely worked out

36. *El Baile de los Gigantes*

respecting the cardinal points and number of steps so as to correspond with Mayan science which underlies the myths. The performers wear masks or veils and tunics with coloured details corresponding with the colours associated with the various gods and cardinal points. The only props are sticks used in fighting and a ball that serves as a severed head, the belly of a pregnant woman, a new-born child, and the object of a battle. The ball has a special significance because from the earliest evidence of Meso-american culture the ball game was associated with the movement of celestial bodies and was a ritual act involving human sacrifice necessary for life.

The performance of this ceremony is intended to counteract the potentially violent effect of the summer solstice when the sun is directly overhead and the concentration of solar energy is the greatest. According to Valdez this tremendous energy can cause a person with spiritual impurities – for example, someone given to anger or envy – to commit violent acts.

So *El Baile de los Gigantes* is a purification for the performers and for the whole tribe as well. It shows the good forces against the bad forces, and by concentrating on the action, the people go through the struggle in a sense and it liberates them from their bad feelings. It is cathartic, but it is also in direct relationship with the Mayan mathematical knowledge of reality.

37. *El Baile de los Gigantes*

The ceremony was created specifically for the Chicano and Latin American Theatre Festival held in Mexico in the summer of 1974. *El Baile de los Gigantes* was presented at noon on 24 June at the pyramids of Teotihuacan. The audience sat on the Pyramid of the Moon and watched the performance down below with the other pyramids as a background. For those of us present it was an impressive occasion and it seemed to us that the performance succeeded in harmonizing the spectators with each other, with mankind, and with the cosmos. The audience joined in singing the final song in Spanish. As they sang, over and over, 'Please god, let the light flourish and come forth', the sacred ball was thrown back and forth from performers to spectators, and many climbed down from the Pyramid and joined performers in a jubilant dance of celebration.

The daily discussions during the Mexico festival made clear the extent of the philosophical and political distance that had come to separate Teatro Campesino from the other Chicano and Latino *teatros,* many of which had originally been modeled after the theatre of Valdez. While the focus of Teatro Campesino was becoming increasingly spiritual, most of the other *teatros* were developing a Marxist consciousness and, through their plays, presenting a social-political analysis in terms of class struggle. They angrily accused Valdez of abandoning his proletarian roots and saw his spirituality as an opiate promoting the *status quo* by refusing to enter into combat against it. The conflicts which Valdez had recognized in his own company and in the Chicano movement, and had written about in plays such as *The Militants,* were present in the festival. The objective of unifying Chicano and Latino cultural workers by emphasizing their common indigenous roots and traditions had failed.

Never again did El Teatro Campesino perform a Mayan ceremony, although on their land in San Juan Bautista at least one Indian marriage ceremony has taken place, and they celebrate Christmas with re-enactments of events surrounding the birth of Christ. Their subsequent major works are less mystical. They combine the acting style developed for the *actos,* some mythological characters from the *mitos,* and elements from a new style called the *corrido.* The original *corridos* were narrative folk ballads often telling stories of love, heroism, and death. In the Teatro performances a small group of musicians sings ballads with new lyrics as narration for the action.

La Carpa de los Rasquachis (The Tent of the Underdogs, 1972) was the first production to use the *corrido* style. The *mito* elements in the play include El Diablo (the Devil), who symbolizes human vices, and La Muerte (a skeleton figure representing death) who, through the use of costume pieces such as a hat or a skirt, plays a variety of characters. The play has undergone many major changes reflecting changes in the focus of the group as well as political circumstances, and the length of the versions had varied from less than an hour to about two hours.

In one of the versions the play begins with a song and procession in which a large banner of the Virgin of Guadalupe is paraded. The Virgin of Guadalupe is a brown-skinned version of the Virgin Mary who appeared as an apparition to a poor Mexican peasant. She has become a religious symbol for Mexican and Chicano Catholics. This is followed by flashes from history showing such events as the conquest of Mexico by the Spaniard Cortes. Most of the play, however, deals with more recent events. La Muerte introduces the story of Jesus Pelado Rasquachi, a Mexican who came to the United States to work in the fields. Throughout his life he wears the rope of a slave around his waist. He falls in love and is married (a priest ropes them together), buys a cheap used car (a tyre which he rolls around the stage), leaves his pregnant wife at home while he gets drunk with La Muerte dressed as a dance-hall girl, comes home and beats his wife who gives birth to seven babies who are baptized by 'Saint Boss Church'. Conditions are tolerable as

38. *La Carpa de los Rasquachis*

39. *La Carpa de los Rasquachis*

40. *La Carpa de los Rasquachis*

41. *La Carpa de los Rasquachis*

long as he is young and strong. When a United Farm Workers organizer comes around, he agrees with his boss that they don't need the union. But suddenly he is forty-seven, worn-out and broke, and he wants to go home to Mexico. His children refuse to go. The skeleton shakes his hand, and he dies, humiliated by the system. The rope he has worn all his life is still around his waist. In one version there is a happy ending. Rasquachi comes back to life, joins the union, and goes on strike

In an earlier version a second act concerns Rasquachi's widow and sons who go to the city where they are caught up in hatred and violence which brings about the deaths of the sons. The final section is a kind of mystical pageant in which the Virgin of Guadalupe appears. One of the sons is transformed into a figure suggesting both Christ and Quetzalcoatl, a Mayan man–god parallel to Christ. We hear, 'You are my other self.' 'If I do harm to you I do harm to myself.' 'Against hatred – love; against violence – peace.'

Despite the apparent pessimism of the story of Rasquachi and his family, the play, even when performed without the final section, is not bitter. The tremendous energy of the performance, the music, the dance, the acrobatic movement, project a positive reaffirmation of life. It is this spirit, without the obvious Mayan and Christian spirituality, that has continued to characterize the work of Teatro Campesino. However, the setting of subsequent plays shifted from the farm to the city, a transition first clearly seen in some versions of *La Carpa de los Rasquachis*.

In *Mundo (World)* the change in focus from *campesinos* to urban Chicanos is complete. Work on this play began in 1972 and was first performed in 1975 as *El Fin del Mundo (The End of the World)*. This highly abstract version, greatly influenced by their Mayan studies, was envisaged as an event for the traditional Mexican celebration of El Dia de los Muertos (The Day of the Dead). The fourth version called *Mundo* (1980), which Valdez considers 'definitive', eliminated the Mayan abstractions and developed urban Chicano characters and an elaborate plot. Although it was no longer considered specifically as a celebration of El Dia de los Muertos, it is permeated by the Mexican concept of death which is a mixture of indigenous and European attitudes. The playwright–director describes the play as a twentieth-century 'Mystery/Miracle play . . . The Mystery is Death, the Miracle is Life.' As with *La Carpa de los Rasquachis, Mundo* combines elements of the *acto* and the *corrido* in its fast-moving *commedia*-like acting, its songs and dance. The *mito* element is still present, but in an altered form. There are no characters borrowed directly from Mayan or Christian mythology, nor is El Diablo or La Muerte present. Instead, all of the characters are human, but with two exceptions their faces are made-up to resemble skulls, and skeletal bones are superimposed on their costumes. The play is set in the world of the dead which parallels the world of the living except that its values are inverted.

In *Mundo* the concept of death is even more central than in previous work. The skeleton figures derive from the Mexican concept that death is not something that can be avoided, which is impossible; instead it is a reminder of the commonality of all people who must eventually die. Material possessions and physical appearances are transitory. Underneath, all people are the same – merely skeletons. From the time of the Mayas, death was thought of as a phase in the cycle of life which is continually being renewed. Human sacrifices were offered to the sun god so that human life could continue. It is a communal rather than an individual view of life.

In *Mundo* we follow Mundo Mata, a kind of urban Chicano Everyman, on his adventures into the other side of reality. There he finds things much the same. His family and friends are living out their deaths as once they had lived out their lives. Mundo's adventures begin with an overdose of heroin. He is being released after serving his 'life' sentence. A jail door is rolled from place to place with Mundo behind it as if going through long corridors. He takes a bus (represented by five women) to the end of the line. Arrested, he is taken to a city jail for the night where he finds his father. His mother he discovers is a prostitute who takes him to her room and to bed in a coffin. Her pimp relieves Mundo of his wallet before he sets out to find his grandparents.

The staging is simple, but the bizarre costumes, the music, dance, and frenetic energy make it seem elaborate. Ten actors play thirty-six characters by changing costume pieces over their skeleton-painted body stockings. Props and two rolling-scaffold units the size of large closets comprise the setting. By rearranging these units they serve as a jail, the Department of Urban Housing Underdevelopment, a hospital, and other locales in the land of the dead. the easy movement from place to place is similar to the jump cuts, segues, and other transitions used in films. Because of these and other cinematic techniques, Valdez refers to the play as a *mono,* a *pachuco* word for movie.

In search of his grandparents Mundo crawls through a tyre and discovers the entire community lying in cemetery-like rows with tyre gravestones at their heads. He comes upon a vendor selling balloons (drugs). Since Mundo has no money he trades his knife for a balloon. The vendor uses it to burst the balloon, scattering glitter which the vendor identifies as 'bone dust' (a reference to the drug called angel dust).

With the help of a street-punk friend who has a bullet hole in his forehead, Mundo finds his pregnant wife Vera at the End of the World Dance. He kills a rival, Little Death, and together he and Vera go to the Department of Unemployment so he can find a job. He has no death certificate for identification, but when he shows them his arm they are so impressed with his 'track record' that they offer him a job as Executive Director of the Drug Abuse Center. Mundo and Vera are in an accident in their low-rider car. At the hospital Mundo is told there is good news and bad news. The bad news is that his wife is alive; the good news is that the baby was born dead. Mundo wants Vera to return to prison with him – that is, back to the world of the living. But Vera refuses to leave her skeleton baby behind.

In the land of the dead characters can be killed over and over. Little

42. *Mundo*

Death, whom Mundo had killed at the dance, attempts to shoot Mundo, but kills Vera instead. The dead Vera wants Mundo to come home with her and the baby, but he is not yet ready to die. 'It's my world,' he says, 'and I'm going to make it survive.' Eventually, skeletons from the land of the dead force him out of their world, and Mundo again finds himself behind bars, sentenced to life. Vera is alive and pregnant. When offered some dust, he refuses. He is through with all of that. He has learned something.

The ironic view of life in the Chicano *barrios* is recognizable through the caricatures and stereotypes. Although *Mundo* concerns working-class people, no specific issue is in focus. The work of El Teatro Campesino has moved further from its identification with the farmworkers' union as it has become concerned with the urban Chicano. This new concern was also evident in *Zoot Suit* (1978), written and directed by Valdez for the Mark Taper Forum in Los Angeles and subsequently produced in new York where it was publicized as the first Chicano play to be presented on Broadway. However, *Zoot Suit* focuses on the historical trial of the 1940s in which seventeen members of a *pachuco* street gang were wrongfully convicted of murder.

Politically-doctrinaire Chicanos and some people identified with the New Left have accused Valdez of selling out because his work is no longer overtly political. It is ironic that in the view of Valdez the failure of *Zoot Suit* in New York was partly because critics perceived it as agitprop theatre. However, he believes that the apparent political advocacy of the play was simply

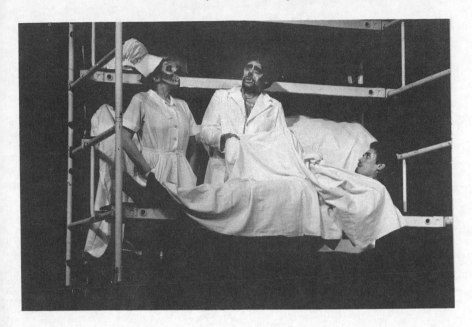

43. *Mundo*

implicit in the historical material. He does not consider the most recent work of the Teatro to be overtly political. The farmworkers are better organized now, there is no acute political cause. Now, according to Valdez, the purpose of their work is to sensitize the public to other aspects of the Mexican people, the history of California, and of the United States. The focus is the Anglo-Hispanic relationship.[7]

None the less, El Teatro Campesino has continued its commitment to the Chicano people as a whole, attempting to avoid divisiveness. And because he is a theatre artist, Valdez is especially concerned about the relationship of Chicanos to the theatre profession. He is convinced that Chicano theatre must establish itself on a professional level – not only for the sake of its artistry, but for the livelihood of its practitioners. The Broadway production of *Zoot Suit* and the projected Hollywood movie are, in his view, in keeping with this objective. Chicanos who have seen El Teatro Campesino, read about its successful European tours, learned that Peter Brook came to spend a summer working with the Teatro in 1973, or that the director of the company was appointed by the Governor to the California Arts Council, now know that it is possible for a Chicano to become a professional theatre artist.

No doubt the early work of El Teatro Campesino in support of the organizing activities of the farmworkers' union was useful especially in persuading scabs to leave the fields, in strengthening the strike, and in helping to make the boycott against non-union grapes and lettuce a success. It is likely, however, the union would have succeeded without the Teatro. The most important contribution of El Teatro Campesino under the leadership of Luis Valdez was the creation of the first Chicano theatre. Since 1965 when his Teatro began, approximately eighty others have been formed. For many of these theatres Teatro Campesino was their model; others, while using the *acto, mito, corrido,* and *mono* styles pioneered by Valdez, focus on specific problems in their own communities and sometimes have a more doctrinaire political perspective.

4
Environmental Theatre

Shortly before sunset spectators on an isolated Pacific beach near San Francisco saw on a distant cliff a giant figure in the form of a young woman standing motionless facing the ocean. After a time she stretched out her arms as if trying to reach something that was beyond the horizon. A squad of military men on a concrete bunker chanted English words in the style of Indonesian music. The words began to appear on white placards placed in long rows on the beach. The words were a letter to the young woman on the cliff written by her dead boyfriend, a sailor overseas during the Second World War.

It was a performance by Snake Theater, but it was taking place in an actual environment, rather than a created one. The young woman and the spectators shared this environment, and there was no clear separation between the real world and the created events. The actual environment was part of the play. The events of the play were happening in the real world and in real time. The beach, the sound of the ocean, the sunset, were all part of the performance and they were also the actual environment experienced by the audience. By contrast, a conventional realistic play happens in a fictional place and time. The theatre building is not a part of the performance and actual time is ignored.

In a perceptual sense, most theatre was environmental before the coming of realism in the nineteenth century. With the techniques of realism, theatre artists attempted to focus the spectator's conscious mind exclusively on fictional illusion so that everything except the world of the characters came to be disregarded. Prior to that time the experience of the audience included the theatrical environment – the theatre décor and architecture, the other

44.   Snake Theater *Somewhere in the Pacific*

spectators, and interaction with other spectators and sometimes with the performers. Because the spectator was conscious of the details making up the theatre experience, he/she actively chose the specific focus at each moment, shifting from a performer on stage to a spectator in one of the boxes to the elaborate décor of the auditorium. Before realism the acting area in British and American theatres projected into the auditorium. So, although the scenery was separated from the auditorium by the proscenium arch, the actors shared the auditorium environment with the audience. With the interest in making the audience focus exclusively on the fictional action, the acting area withdrew behind the proscenium arch, the box set placed performers within the scenery rather than in front of it, the auditorium lights were darkened during the performance so as to exclude from consciousness everything that was not on stage, and the audience behaviour became passive. The environment which surrounded the spectator was no longer part of the performance experience. Neither were the other spectators as each was expected to relate solely to the fictional world on the other side of an invisible wall.

The American happenings beginning in the late 1950s, and many of the productions of the alternative theatres which followed, revived the earlier perceptual relationship of spectator to environment. They created performances which the audience perceived as sharing their environment. When the San Francisco Mime Troupe performs in a park, even though they use scenery to suggest the place of the fictional action, the audience is very much aware of the park as the environment for the performers, the scenery, the other spectators, and themselves. The spectators interact with each other and the performers acknowledge the audience. The Living Theatre, in such works as *Paradise Now* and *Prometheus,* not only share the same environment, they intermingle during parts of the performances and some spectators participate in the action.

The physical surroundings for environmental performances can be divided roughly into (1) found environments such as that used for the Snake Theater production on the beach, and (2) constructed environments made for specific productions such as those directed by Richard Schechner for the Performance Group. In both instances, the first principle of environmental theatre is that the performers and audience share the same environment even if they stay in separate parts of it.

Richard Schechner
The Performance Group

The Performance Group was formed in New York by Richard Schechner in 1967 to experiment with environmental theatre, group process, training techniques, and the performer–audience relationship.[1] Schechner, a professor at New York University's School of the Arts, was interested in performance theory and had formulated '6 Axioms for Environmental Theatre'[2] published in *The Drama Review* which he edited.

These axioms are most helpful in understanding Schechner's production intentions: (1) It is necessary to accept a definition of theatre which is not based upon traditional distinctions between life and art. (2) 'All the space is used for performance' and 'all the space is used for audience'. (3) 'The theatrical event can take place either in a totally transformed space or in "found space".' (4) 'Focus is flexible and variable.' In environmental theatre the focus can be single as in the traditional theatre, or 'multi-focus' where the space is arranged so that the spectator cannot see everything without moving or refocusing and more than one event takes place at the same time, forcing the spectator to choose which to observe. Or there can be a 'local focus' where only a fraction of the audience can perceive the event. (5) 'One element is not submerged for the sake of others.' The performer is no more important than the other audible and visual elements. Sometimes performers may be 'treated as mass and volume, color, texture, and movement'. (6) 'The text need be neither the starting point nor the goal of a production. There may be no text at all.'

Schechner's environmental ideas deepened through practice, and a few years later culminated in his book on *Environmental Theatre* (1973). But his six axioms express his understanding at the time the Performance Group began work on the first of the three productions which did the most to explore the concept–*Dionysus in 69* (1968), *Makbeth* (1969), and *Commune* (1970).

There is another concept, relating specifically to acting, which had an impact on these productions. About the same time as Schechner's early workshops, Jerzy Grotowski was giving workshops at the University. When Schechner interviewed him Grotowski commented that he had observed in the United States a certain 'external friendliness' which was part of the 'daily mask'. 'There are qualities of behaviour in every country that one must break through in order to create. Creativity does not mean using our daily masks but rather to make exceptional situations where our daily masks do not function.'[3] Like Grotowski, in his work with the Performance Group Schechner wanted the actors to go beyond the mask, to become vulnerable.

The company found an empty garage on Wooster Street which became the Performing Garage. Michael Kirby, known for his work with happenings and later editor of *The Drama Review* and founder of the Structuralist Workshop, collaborated with Jerry Rojo in designing the environment for *Dionysus in 69.* In the empty space–approximately 15 metres by 11 metres with a height of 6 metres – they constructed several wooden towers with as many as five levels. These were arranged around the perimeter of the room. The audience sat on the floor or climbed to one of the levels. The centre floor was left open for the principal acting area, but the performers also used the towers, and the spectators could move into the central area when they wished. This arrangement of space had been suggested by an outdoor exercise which ended on the rooftop of a nearby building.

A book by the company, edited by Schechner, documents the development of *Dionysus in 69* in text and photos.[4] Soon after the workshops began, the exercises focused upon *The Bacchae* of Euripides. When the production opened they were using fewer than half of the lines of the play plus a few from *Hippolytus* and *Antigone.* The text for the remainder of the three-hour performance was made by the performers who wrote their own dialogue or developed it during workshops or rehearsals throughout the run.

Euripides' play deals with Dionysus, the god of wine, drunkenness, revelry, freedom from restrictions. He has arrived in Thebes to spread his worship, but is resisted by King Pentheus who opposes the irrational behaviour of the cult. Dionysus has roused the women of the city to emotional frenzy in the celebration of his rites. Even the blind seer Teiresias and Cadmus, the grandfather of Pentheus, are drunk. Pentheus arrests Dionysus as the leader of this debauchery, but the god gradually puts him under his spell, makes him drunk. Behaving like a female Bacchant Pentheus goes off to the mountains where the women are celebrating. A little later a Messenger arrives and describes how the frenzied women, led by Agave, the mother of Pentheus, tore the King to pieces believing him to be a wild beast. Agave enters with the head of her son. Gradually she regains her sense and comes to realize what she has done. Dionysus arrives and announces that the entire family of Pentheus will be punished.

In the Performance Group's production actors simultaneously played Euripides' characters and themselves, much as was being done by the Living

45. *Dionysus in 69*, **photo: Frederich Eberstadt**

Theatre. Dionysus was not only referred to as the god, but by the name of the actor playing the role. And that actor not only used some of Euripides' speeches, but also some that he improvised or had developed. This meant that some parts of the production were different each night, and it put focus on the presence of the actors more than on the fictional characters.

Several sections were devised which put focus on the bodies of the performers. The physicality of the birth of Dionysus was increased midway through the run when the entire cast began performing it in the nude. The actor playing Dionysus tells the audience some of the facts concerning his own birth and then excuses himself so that he can go to be born. The men lie side by side facing the floor. Above them stand the women, one behind another, legs spread forming a kind of birth canal. Dionysus lies across the backs of the men, between the legs of the women, surrounded by flesh, and is moved along by contraction-like movements of the men's backs and the

95

arms and legs of the women until finally he emerges and rolls into the lap of the closest spectator.

The birth ritual is followed by a dance of celebration which involves those members of the audience willing to participate. The tempo slowly increases and the dance continues to develop until it becomes ecstatic. Finally, it is interrupted when William Shephard as Pentheus climbs to the top of one of the highest towers and, speaking over a bullhorn, admonishes the Bacchants to return to their homes.

Pentheus has Dionysus put in the pit in the floor of the garage. In Euripides' text Dionysus revenges this imprisonment by humiliating Pentheus, but in the Performance Group production this mortification is not of Pentheus but of actor Shephard. The scene came from workshop encounter exercises. Each performer asks Shephard a question which is difficult to answer and personally revealing. The scene continues until Shephard is unable to answer. Once the questioning went on for more than an hour.

Dionysus says he can give Shephard any woman in the room. Shephard says he does not need Dionysus, and to prove it he goes into the audience, finds a woman whom he caresses and kisses. He tries to make love with her but is usually resisted. Once Shephard left with a woman at this point and did not return. If he fails, Dionysus says he can help, but first Shephard must make love to him. After a kiss, the two go into the pit where Pentheus is to be further humiliated by being forced to make love to Dionysus. The humiliation is not only of the character but also of the actor, and it becomes the equivalent of Euripides having Pentheus put on the clothes of a female Bacchant.

After the two go into the pit, the other performers move into the audience and select individuals to caress. It becomes a group caress nearly identical to that of 'The Rite of Universal Intercourse' in the Living Theatre's *Paradise Now* which opened in France the following month. As performers and spectators lie intertwined on the floor, stroking, hugging, and kissing each other, Dionysus and Pentheus come out of the pit and watch. Gradually the caresses become scratches and the kisses bites, eventually leading to the scene of Pentheus' death. Again the men lie on their faces with the women standing above them, legs spread. Pentheus goes back into the womb. It is his death; the women's hands, dipped in blood, are held over his head. By the end of the ritual blood is everywhere.

The production ran for 163 performances over more than a year and was continually being evaluated and changed. During most of this time there were six men and four women performers. After a couple of months the group decided to rotate some of the roles so that the production and performers could grow. Dionysus was played at different times by three men and a woman, Pentheus by two men, Teiresias by a man and a woman.

The Performance Group workshops had begun by using some of Grotowski's psycho-physical exercises involving imagination and body. A few of these and other workshop exercises subsequently served as public

46. *Dionysus in 69*, **photo: Raeanne Rubenstein**

warm-up exercises, and others were incorporated into such sections as the mortification of Pentheus and the audience caress. But Grotowski had devised the exercises for the purpose of training actors and felt that they had no meaning as performance. Furthermore, he distrusted group improvisation and considered it a peculiarly American addiction which removed responsibility from individual performers by immersing them in what he called 'the warm waters of family relations'.[5]

Using exercises in performance was one means of focusing on the actors by exposing them without the mask of character. The potential vulnerability was increased by incorporating sections in which performers talked about themselves, responded as themselves, and interacted with spectators whose actions could not be precisely anticipated. Nakedness was another means of increasing psychic vulnerability. The elimination of clothing removed from the performer one of the chief social means of masking oneself. By exposing the body, some inner mental, muscular, and visceral processes became visible which helped to emphasize the actual performer rather than a fictional character. Although nudity was not again used as extensively as in *Dionysus in 69*, the Performance Group continued their interest in work which was performer-centred rather than character-centred.

The title of their next production, *Makbeth,* as in the Germanized spelling of *Amerika,* let the audience know they should not expect Shakespeare's play. By associating the play with Germany, audiences in 1969 might also assume that it had something to do with fascism. The company began working

97

on the production in autumn 1968, not long after the Democratic Party Convention in Chicago where the demonstrations of idealistic young people were confronted by the over-reactions of police in what many saw as a direct reflection of an autocratic government. The Performance Group had decided their new play would be concerned with fascism in the United States.

Schechner says that the group restructured Shakespeare's test, using it as a plasterer uses plaster. The nine characters in the production were divided into four categories. The *Doers* were Makbeth and Lady Makbeth', the *Victims/Founders* were Duncan and Banquo, the *Avengers* were Malcolm and Macduff, and the *Dark Powers,* of course, were the three witches. Duncan's children – including Malcolm, Macduff and Banquo – want to get rid of him and he hopes Makbeth will protect him. But at the first banquet Duncan is served as food to the children and the Makbeths. The plot generally follows Shakespeare except that at the end Malcolm has Macduff killed and goes off trying to eat the crown.

The space within the Performing Garage was redesigned for the production. The audiences (about seventy-five people) were free to move around in the space during the performance like unseen members of the court, hiding in corners and tiptoeing in stockinged feet from one shadow to another secretly to observe and overhear. There were stairways, ladders, a ramp, a trench, a vertical grandstand of five storeys, and cubes two and three storeys high comprising a labyrinthine environment.

Schechner has described the performance as occurring throughout the space, often with three or four scenes playing simultaneously.[6] There was no place from which a spectator could see everything. The murder of Banquo took place under a platform and was seen by only a few. When the Dark Powers made their prophecy in the trench fifty spectators stood or crouched around it. Sometimes spectators were included in the action. They gathered around a low central platform which served as the table for the banquet scene, and a few joined in the procession which was both Duncan's funeral cortège and Makbeth's coronation parade. Although, in general, the audience had the same experience, it varied somewhat depending upon the location of each spectator. The environment was not designed for a conformity of reactions.

A new environment was constructed for *Commune* which opened in December 1970. (After changes and a reduction in the number of performers it became *Commune 2* and then *Commune 3.*) This production was also developed through group improvisations. However, it did not make use of a script as a starting point. Instead, the mythic element came from events in American history, ancient and recent, from literary works such as *Moby Dick* and the Bible, from politics, and from folk songs and spirituals. The environment for this collage was a wooden construction consisting of platforms, ladders, catwalks, a vertical grandstand, a large tub, and a rolling floor which suggested an ocean, rolling plains, or a roller coaster.

The production centres on the killing of film actress Sharon Tate and her

47. *Makbeth*, **photo: Frederich Eberstadt**

friends by members of the Charles Manson commune, and on the My Lai
massacre by American soldiers in Vietnam. The two events, Schechner says,
were understood by the company as 'rather identical incidents of national
policy'.[7] The characters are young people who, like the Manson group, seek
Utopia in California's Death Valley. In so doing they act out American
history, including the sailing to the New World, the race across the conti-
nent, the killing of Indians, serving in the army, and vacationing in the
Virgin Islands. Schechner says these scenes are performed as they might
have been acted out by members of the commune the night after the Tate
murders.

The Performance Group attempted in the production to develop non-
manipulative ways of including the audience in the action. As the audience
enters they are asked to remove their shoes and place them on a blanket
where a large pile is accumulating. The performers are already in the room

dressed in costumes from a used clothing store. One of the two women performers walks among the spectators asking if they have anything they would like to burn and collecting bits of paper in a metal container. Later these are burned and become the camp fire in one of the scenes.

The audience is aware of the performance beginning when about a dozen people, including five of the performers, line up and one of the women points out those whom she is accusing. The sailing of the Mayflower with the colonists is suggested by performer-created sounds – the sea, wind, creaking ship, and seagulls. The ship arrives at the Statue of Liberty represented by one of the women who recites the inscription in a Brooklyn accent. Actors evoke the mood of Death Valley at night by howling like coyotes. Other scenes include a western movie gun fight that is predominantly comic until one of the participants is killed, and the arrival of one of the women at the commune. The newcomer, Clementine, is timid but gradually she comes to trust the others and with their help she flies. The other woman, blindfolded, searches for El Dorado as she wanders among the audience asking people for their help.

Near the end of the performance Lt Calley gives testimony on the slaughter of Vietnamese at My Lai. As he tells how men, women, and children were herded together and shot, other performers drag the pile of shoes to the centre of the environment. Wearing shoes chosen from the pile the performers approach the 'white house on the hill' to murder the inhabitants, including the pregnant Sharon Tate. The performance ends with a section called 'Possibilities' in which the actors wash themselves in the large tub and the spectators retrieve their shoes as they talk to one another and to the performers.

Commune is concerned not only with dropping out and violence, but also with American concepts of ownership. Hippies take from the established society because, as one performer says, 'Everything belongs to everybody.' During the performance various objects are taken from the reluctant audience, and when Clementine's self-image changes after adapting to the commune, she changes clothes with a spectator. The hesitancy of the audience in giving up these items stands for the larger preoccupation of Americans concerning property. The members of the commune do not escape this obsession any more than the middle-class audience. Their fantasy is to have dune buggies for everyone. They are all infected with the American dream.

However, the production also functions in a non-metaphorical way. It is a means of interaction between performers and spectators. Schechner believes that such interaction is essential in fulfilling what people need from the theatre – a narrative structure which provides an opportunity for exchange between people. Parties can provide this exchange without the narrative; cinema and traditional twentieth-century theatre provide the narrative without the exchange. Some have considered the interaction at the end of the play to be the most important because it creates a potential for

48. *Commune*

change.[8] The importance of interaction to the company is suggested by the fact that they pronounce *Commune* as a verb, with the accent on the second syllable, rather than as a noun.

The first three productions of the Performance Group had explored the principle techniques of the environmental theatre concept as it was being formulated by Schechner. Those works which followed had less to explore even though they were significant artistic achievements. In *The Tooth of Crime* (1972) Schechner worked with a new script by Sam Shepard. *Mother Courage and Her Children* (1974) was an environmental production of Brecht's play. *The Marilyn Project* (1975) used a script by David Gaard who worked daily with the group. In the next two productions the acting area and the audience were separate and distinct. *Oedipus* (1977), Ted Hughes's adaptation of Seneca, was presented in a miniature coliseum with dirt floor and steeply-raked seating built inside the Performing Garage. In *Cops* (1978), by Terry Curtis Fox, the audience looked down from two sides into the hyper-real environment of a functioning diner. The last Performance Group production directed by Schechner was Genet's *The Balcony* (1979) where, like the first three productions of the company, the acting areas were among the spectators.

Schechner had chosen as members of the Performance Group strong individuals who would have an impact on the work through their unique contri-

49. *Mother Courage and Her Children*

butions. As the unifying external forces dissipated with the ending of the
Vietnam war, the energy that had been focused on social rebellion became
focused on individual artistic expression. Schechner wanted to continue
creating works which were expansive, which like Asian theatre and Western
classics create an entire world. Spalding Gray, on the other hand, had a
narcissistic focus and wanted to work with Elizabeth LeCompte in developing productions which explored his own life. Eventually, Schechner's work
and the work of Gray and LeCompte could not be accommodated within the
same company. The performer–collaborators in the company could not be
committed to both, and economically two companies were impossible.
Schechner withdrew from active participation in 1980 and began to direct
individual projects elsewhere and to spend more time writing. Gray and
LeCompte, together with several other members of the company – Jim Clayburgh, Willem Dafoe, Libby Howes, and Ron Vawter – took over the
Performing Garage and became the Wooster Group, named for the street
where the Garage is located.

Under Schechner's direction the Performance Group adapted techniques
and concepts from several sources and made them their own. The concept of
environmental theatre had already been revived by the producers of happenings; exercises were borrowed from Grotowski and used, with changes,
in performance. Some of the techniques of group therapy, sensitivity train-

50. *Cops*

ing, and encounter groups were used in workshops. The Living Theatre and others had used classics as the starting point for collective works; simultaneity of scenes, audience participation, and improvisation had been used by the producers of happenings and by the Living Theatre. The Living Theatre had also used the technique of actors playing themselves. While the use of these techniques and the formulation of these concepts pre-dated the Performance Group, they were not simply borrowed by Schechner. They were thoroughly explored through practice and their understanding deepened through his writing.

Schechner's objective had been to develop through practice a theory of performance that was separate from the theory of texts. The key to this goal he found in environmental thinking. The fundamental principle of environmental theatre is to begin with an empty space, without a preconception of where the audience or the performers will be or how they will relate. These are developed as part of the rehearsal. Thus environmental theatre, according to Schechner, deals with whole worlds – not merely fragments placed in spaces predetermined by convention.

The Bread and Puppet Theater

When Peter Schumann founded the Bread and Puppet Theater in New York in 1961 he initiated the practice of sharing with the audience dark bread which he made from hand-ground flour. Schumann believes that theatre

103

should be as basic to life as bread. Some of his productions have been made for outdoor found environments where a carnival-like atmosphere is created involving as many as a hundred participants. Others have been designed for presentation by a few performers on sidewalks or indoors.

In Munich in 1959 Schumann had begun to introduce large sculptured bodies into dance performances. After moving to the United States, the productions always used puppets, some as tall as five metres, in combination with masked performers. The performances are predominantly visual, in the mode of popular entertainment accessible to everyone. The atmosphere is informal, the style projects an apparent child-like simplicity, and there is a spirit of gentleness which evokes a sense of community among the spectators. The performances, varying in length from a few minutes to three hours, sometimes use banners, painted backcloths, 'crankies' which tell a story through pictures drawn on a roll of paper which passes from one roller to another, folk music – both instrumental and vocal – and may involve a procession or parade. By 1981 Schumann had created well over a hundred productions.

While the intention of the Bread and Puppet Theater is not to advocate a political doctrine, Schumann's work is a protest against the dehumanizing effects of modern urban life and its materialism. He wants to evoke in his audiences a direct emotional response to those forces which promote destruction of the human spirit.

A fifteen-minute play such as *The King's Story* (first version 1963) could be presented outdoors without prearrangement, or with other short plays as an entire indoor programme. The staging requirements for this parable are especially simple. A red cloth about two metres high is attached to a pole on each side. One pole is held erect by the narrator, the other by a trumpeter. As the narrator tells the story, it is enacted by rod puppets visible above the cloth who use non-verbal vocal sounds. The story is punctuated by drum, trumpet and cymbals. One puppet, the Great Warrior, is a tall puppet with a man inside who walks in front of the red cloth carrying two swords. The Great Warrior comes into the King's country offering his services, but the King sends him away. When a Dragon appears, however, the people and the King are afraid. Ignoring the advice of his counsellors – a Priest, a Red Man, and a Blue Man and his Son – the King sends for the Great Warrior who kills the Dragon, then he kills the King and his counsellors, and then he kills the People. The Great Warrior is alone. And then Death comes and kills the Great Warrior.

Schumann is a pacifist and consequently many of the works he created during the Vietnam war were protests against such inhumanity. *A Man Says Goodbye to His Mother* (1968), 'a sidewalk show', is presented by three performers using simple gestures and only a few props. A narrator wearing a death mask prepares a young man for war as a woman wearing a white mask representing his mother looks on. The young man 'goes to a country far away . . . It is a very dangerous country.' The narrator gives the young man a gun,

51. *The King's Story*

a gas mask, and a toy aeroplane. The narrator tells us that the man comes to a village in a foreign land. The woman exchanges her white mask for a black one. 'The man takes his aeroplane to look for his enemy.' (The man moves the toy plane as if it were flying.) 'The people are afraid.' (The woman cringes as drum and trumpet sound.) 'The man is afraid.' (The man covers his eyes.) The man poisons the crops, he burns a house, he bombs the children. The woman's arm guided by the narrator representing death, kills the young man with a pair of scissors. The woman changes back to the original mask, and the narrator presents a letter to her which says, 'We regret to inform you.'

Many of Schumann's productions have a mythological atmosphere, and many borrow stories, images, or characters from religious sources. *The Cry of the People for Meat* (1969) draws upon the Bible, presenting images from the creation of the world to the crucifixion. The material taken from the Old Testament depicts a corrupt society of imperialism and violence. Christ is shown resisting these powers and attempting to create a new order devoid of materialism and corruption. The parallels in our own times are underlined by the interjection of contemporary images.

Until 1970 the group centred its work in New York City, with extensive tours in Europe. In 1970 Peter Schumann, his family, and a few puppeteers became a theatre-in-residence at Goddard College in Plainfield, Vermont, where they lived and worked at Cate Farm. In 1974 this group disbanded and Schumann and his family moved to another farm near Glover, Vermont. They work this farm themselves without the help of motorized machinery. They raise animals and grain and make maple syrup from the trees on the farm. From time to time Schumann invites those with whom he wants to work to come to Vermont to do a specific project which might subsequently tour to Europe. Schumann himself is invited to universities and other institutions where he works with students and others in the community for a specific period of time on a specific project. However, a kind of continuity is pro vided by a recurring project, *The Domestic Resurrection Circus,* first presented in 1970, and created anew each summer since 1974 in a meadow on the Vermont farm.

Past members of the company come to Vermont from throughout the United States and Europe, bringing their own shows and helping to build the figures and masks designed by Schumann for *The Domestic Resurrection Circus.* The director and performers then explore the appropriate movements of the figures they have built – giant puppets, flocks of birds, herds of deer or horses, clowns, and masked figures. A period of musical experimentation follows, and finally a narrative is developed by Schumann from the elements which have emerged. The performers are not actors, they use the puppets, masks, and 'crankies' to demonstrate a story. The performance of the multi-focused work lasts most of the day. Peter Schumann has explained why the *Circus* is presented at the farm.

> It's a piece that shouldn't be traveled, something we want to perform where we can integrate the landscape, that we can do with real time and real rivers and mountains and animals. It's something that is seen in the woods, up there in the hills, back here in the river. I guess it would be called an 'environment'.[9]

In the spring of 1975 Schumann was invited to the University of California at Davis where he made a production for a very different outdoor environment. The site he chose was an excavation for a building that had not been built. The excavation, partially covered with weeds, was approximately eighty-eight metres by sixty-three metres and was surrounded on all sides by mounds of earth about seven metres high. During a two-week period, with the help of more than sixty students, faculty, and townspeople, he made an entire parade and 'anti-bicentennial pageant' dedicated to Ishi, the last member of a northern Californian tribe of American Indians. The theme had been chosen by Schumann because of the approaching American bicentennial (1976) and his feeling that Americans of European heritage should understand their own celebration in the light of their forerunners' tragedy.[10] His idea was not to create a historical illustration of the tragedy, 'but a free-form work on the inherent theme: peace of the Indians, war of the whites'.

When Schumann arrived to begin work, he had only a vague idea of the form it should take. Upon seeing the outdoor environment, he abandoned even that idea as not suited to the terrain. By the following morning, he had formulated a new structure and principal images for the work and had made some notes and sketches. It would begin with a parade through the town and campus, ending at the excavation site where the pageant would be presented. In a general meeting he described the project and explained that during the day participants would be building masks, costumes, and banners, and in the evening rehearsing movement and music.

In the following two weeks, with the help of the group, Schumann designed and made thirty-six Deer masks and costumes with tree branches for antlers, twenty-one Butchers' costumes with black top hats and beards, twenty hardboard printing blocks from which over fifty flags and banners were printed, sixteen masks and costumes for Hunchback Witches, and four establishment Gods ranging in height up to four metres mounted on two carts pulled by Dragons. Schumann designed each of these items and demonstrated how to make them. As he continued to work at designing or building, he also supervised the work of others.

In the evening rehearsals Schumann directed the music of a small band assembled from the participants, conducted the singing, or rehearsed the movement of the Deer and Butchers. Schumann worked from eight in the morning until past ten in the evening. Others worked when they could.

The anti-bicentennial pageant, *A Monument for Ishi,* was performed once at sundown on 23 May 1975. It was preceded by a parade through the town consisting of a small truck with a piano and a piano player, Peter Schumann on one-and-a-half metre stilts, several clowns with a baby carriage, a two-wheeled cart pulled by a Dragon which had two Gods mounted on top and eight Hunchback Witches surrounding it, twenty-one Butchers who walked in two orderly columns carrying flags, another two-wheeled cart with Gods surrounded by eight more Hunchback Witches, the San Francisco Mime Troupe Band, about thirty banners carried by participants, and finally one Deer and a little girl walking together. The girl carried a sign saying 'A Monument for Ishi'.

When the parade arrived at the performance site, the spectators stood or sat on an earth mound on one side of the excavation facing into the setting sun. The two carts from the parade were placed in the excavation so that the Gods appeared to be observing the performance.

The Clowns announce the beginning of the performance and the San Francisco Mime Troupe Band plays as the Clowns do tricks. One of the Clowns rings a large bell signalling the entrance of the Deer and Butchers. There are no more words spoken. A herd of thirty-six Deer, each with a performer inside, enters the excavation in slow motion. When they reach the centre, twenty-one Butchers with their flags flying appear on top of the mounds on the three sides where there is no audience. A bugle is heard and other bugles answer at various distances. The Butchers run down from the top of the mounds and surround the Deer, running in a circle around them with flags flying. A large bell is rung and the Butchers stop. Eight people with horns made of plastic pipe and the neck-half of plastic bottles form a circle around the Deer inside the circle of the Butchers. The horns make a

52. *A Monument for Ishi*

53. *A Monument for Ishi*

54. *A Monument for Ishi*

55. *A Monument for Ishi*

moaning sound as the Deer mill around their centre pivot in slow motion for perhaps three minutes before they lie down.

The large bell is rung again and the Butchers stop waving their flags and hold them as high as possible as a lone figure in black enters. He moves slowly and deliberately from one Deer to another, breaking the wooden antlers as the sound of the horns continues. When all the antlers are broken, the figure walks away and the horn blowers stop blowing and also leave. The Butchers lower their flags and rest the poles on the ground.

One of the Clowns walks to the pile of Deer bodies and realizes that they are dead. He runs sobbing loudly to the chief Clown who blows his whistle and organizes the Clowns into a military formation. He blows his whistle again, signalling the truck with its piano to move in toward the Deer. The Clowns dig a small hole in which they plant a tiny U.S. flag on a two-metre pole. The piano plays an *arpeggio* as the flag is raised. The Clowns salute as the 'national anthem', represented by a simple Bach piece, is played on the piano.

The large bell is rung and Peter Schumann on stilts, dressed as Lady Resurrection and wearing a mask, enters the excavation. He dances to the music of the four-piece band of recorders and flute. At the end of the dance Lady Resurrection bows and the Clowns bow in return, and she signals to the Clowns to distribute wings to the Deer. One of the Clowns puts on a costume painted blue with white clouds. The Butchers have disappeared. As Lady Resurrection dances, a Clown taps on the head of each Deer and the person inside comes out to receive a pair of diaphanous wings. The winged people form a group, and when all of the Deer have been resurrected and Lady Resurrection has exited, they sing three hymns. When the hymns have been sung, Schumann re-enters without his stilts and passes out bread and aïoli to the spectators who came down from the mound into the excavation. There is an exhilarating spirit of community as they eat and talk until twilight turns to dusk.

By 1978, in addition to the Schumanns, there was a full-time nucleus of four living on the farm and creating touring productions. Such a production was *Ave Maris Stella* (1978), using the medieval mass by Josquin des Pres which was sung by the Word of Mouth Chorus. However, the production is not a religious event, but a humanist one in keeping with all of Schumann's work. Images are drawn from the Old as well as the New Testament and other legends. Mary is the central figure who survives the calamities of the centuries including expulsion from Paradise and the Flood. Although there is a procession through the audience and performers serve bread to the spectators, most of the performance takes place on a platform stage and is viewed from one perspective. This arrangement was necessary to accommodate the elaborate visual production including painted drops and puppets of many sizes which are pulled on from the wings or lowered from above.

Myths from many cultures work on Schumann's imagination, producing

56. *A Monument for Ishi*

57. *A Monument for Ishi*

stories and puppets which have the simplicity and power of archetypes. It is his objective to make the puppets and masks directly expressive rather than using them as symbols. The movement of each puppet is carefully explored so as to make it expressive as in dance but outside of dance convention. It is the intent of direct emotive expression that makes words in these productions of secondary importance and dictates that they be used with poetic economy. The lighting serves a similar purpose whether provided by electric torches, candles, daylight, or theatrical lighting instruments. Although in general the plays may be concerned with social issues, they do not preach, they do not present social analyses, nor are they concerned with solving problems. Instead they deal with elemental human themes presented without ideological comment. They are not sentimental, but assertive in their humanism.

Peter Schumann has spoken of the *Domestic Resurrection Circus* as demonstrating the whole world. Each work creates a unique world that is complete, rather than presenting a fragment of everyday life following theatrical conventions and set in a space where the audience–performer relationship has been predetermined. Schumann attempts to avoid performing in traditional theatres because the audience's reaction is conditioned by what they expect to take place in such spaces. Instead, the Bread and Puppet Theater performs in a variety of non-theatrical spaces where the performance dominates the space rather than the other way around. In each environment they use all of the space. The performers are not confined to a specific area although there may be one or more principal performing areas. The physical relationship between spectator and performer varies with each venue.

This principle of inclusiveness applies not only to space, but also to the audience. The popular entertainment techniques of puppetry and circus are not exclusive; they can be enjoyed by all ages, classes, and sensibilities. Schumann strives to make the performances clear, concentrated, and precise. He says 'theatre is good when it makes sense to people'. If a five-year-old can understand it, so will the adults.[11] Furthermore, Bread and Puppet productions are intended to include the spectator in a community made up of performers and other spectators rather than aiming for individual psychic involvement in a fictional world to the extent that the audience is unaware of the actual world of performers and spectators. In part, the awareness of performers is accomplished by the use of story-telling techniques – narration and puppets – where performers are narrators or puppeteers. They are not to be taken as characters but as themselves. The communal relationship is aided by making the spectators active participants. They are always invited to share bread with the performers, and in some productions such as *The Domestic Resurrection Circus* or *A Monument for Ishi* many spectators are also performers. Even carrying a banner in a procession increases one's stake in the community of celebrants.

Schumann believes that 'art is by now what religion used to be. It is . . . the form for the communal event, the shape of the celebrations that we might have with each other'.[12] Peter Schumann is not only the designer of these celebrations, he also officiates. He makes both the performance and the bread; he invites the audience to share both with the performers and each other. It is a celebration of the humanity they have in common.

The work of the Bread and Puppet Theater has influenced and stimulated theatre workers in America and Europe. They have been impressed by the techniques and unpretentiousness of the productions, by Schumann's commitment, and by his simple life style which lacks the usual separation of life and art. Art is his life. Groups emulating his work have been started by former members of the company as far afield as Germany and California.

Snake Theater

Snake Theater in California has used commonplace situations, sometimes created for found environments, and developed them into productions of epic dimensions. Their plays have concerned a waitress in an all-night cafe, a sailor and the girl he left behind, and a family whose car broke down in a gas station. The performers wear bold sculpted masks, and they use carefully designed props, paintings, puppets, and figures of all sizes which sometimes have live performers inside. Their theatre is a visual experience rather than a psychological one. Masks convey character directly and help put focus on the visual elements rather than on the inner needs of characters. Laura Farabough and Christopher Hardman, who formed the theatre in 1972 as the Beggars' Theater, trained in the visual arts and they set out to create a visual theatre. They think of puppets and live performers as moving sculptures, and of the performance as a painting animated by movement.

Hardman had worked with Peter Schumann of the Bread and Puppet Theater. Like Schumann's, the early work of Hardman and Farabough incorporated mythological themes and characters, and in a general way was concerned with social issues. Being interested in folk art and ethnic music, they set out to create a cycle of plays relating to the seasons, which would be in harmony with folk beliefs throughout the world. Subsequent productions, however, revealed a growing interest in using Californian environments while retaining a concern with the techniques of other cultures. They developed their own unique style based on everyday events and characters. In part the change was the result of two additions to the group in 1977 – Lary Graber, a composer and musician who combined Asian musical forms with electronics, and his wife Evelyn Lewis, who has a modern dance background and a strong interest in Indonesian dance. From 1977 until Graber's death in 1980 the four permanent members of the company studied Javanese mask dancing which greatly influenced the movement in their productions. After Graber died, the name Snake Theater was no longer used. Hardman and Farabough formed separate companies, Antenna and Nightfire, each with a distinct method and style.

The aesthetic of Snake Theater derived from the experience of its members in visual arts, music and dance, which helped the company avoid the pitfalls of episodic structure and the common-denominator principle which have plagued some other collectives. The four permanent members assumed specific responsibilities which arose from their particular skills. Farabough and Hardman shared the script writing, which tended to begin with visual ideas. The scripts, including Hardman's drawings, were then shown to Graber and Lewis for their reactions, and the four discussed the mood of the music, the masks, and props. Then Graber would compose the music, Hardman would design the masks and props, and Farabough and Lewis together would direct the movement of the performers. All four were involved in the productions, often as musicians or actors.

Snake Theater's productions were on two different scales. They created intimate performances which could tour to conventional performance spaces using a maximum of four or five performers, and they made elaborate productions with large casts for specific found spaces. Regardless of scale, the plays were set in California and presented stories of commonplace events which became extraordinary through a style that removed them from realism. The actors did not speak, instead their fragmented thoughts were on tape, or spoken by performers offstage, or projected as captions on a screen. The figures, wearing sculptural masks or mask-like make-up, moved in ways carefully developed to put specific characteristics into focus. Live music – vocal and instrumental – composed and conducted by Graber, helped imbue the events with a mood.

In the plays created for found environments, the company sometimes began with the mood that the place suggested. The site chosen for *Somewhere in the Pacific* (1978), a beach and cliffs at the Marin headlands near San Francisco, evoked in the company a feeling of yearning for something far away. They invented the story of Carole, a young woman represented by a puppet three metres tall, who stands on a distant cliff facing the ocean. Except for raising her arms, she is motionless throughout the performance as she awaits the return of her sailor boyfriend Ryan, who is with the navy somewhere in the Pacific during the Second World War. The narrative element is a letter written by Ryan to Carole which she receives after his death. The words used in the performance are from this letter.

The performance begins about an hour before sunset. As the giant Carole looks toward the horizon from her cliff, musicians dressed in army combat uniforms chant 'Chevrolet' which we learn later is from the letter. The vocal and instrumental music, based on Gregorian and Balinese chants, continues throughout the performance. General and Mrs MacArthur stroll down the beach and sit at a table listening to a radio playing sounds of the ocean, which competes with the real ocean sounds. The Sailor Ryan sits at the water's edge writing a letter. The words appear on placards which attendants place in the sand. Later, when only phrases from the letter are left on the beach, they take on other meanings. 'I shall return' is Ryan's promise to Carole and

58.   *Somewhere in the Pacific*

it was General MacArthur's vow to return to the Pacific. MacArthur rises from the table and goes to the ocean. The placards spell out 'The sun is going down', and indeed it is setting. General MacArthur fires a flare pistol at the sun and it goes down.

The performance is much richer than the simple romantic story of Carole and Ryan because the repetition of carefully selected images gives multiple meanings to the narrative. At first the narrative fragments sung by the musicians have value only as musical sound, but as time passes the phrases in both aural and visual form relate to Carole and Ryan, to General Mac-Arthur, to abstract feelings of yearning, and to the actual environment in which the spectators are present. Indeed, the intermingling of actual elements in the environment with created elements contributes much to the complexity of the work. There is the actual sound of the ocean as well as the recorded ocean coming from MacArthur's radio. A real ship passes. A giant puppet looks at the ocean. The letter, revealed on placards, is as important for its visual presence as for its narrative information.

Laura Farabough says that their work had a surface of 'here and now'. They 'present the audience with a story line and then suddenly erase it, making the audience conscious of the fact that it's a real ocean out there, they are actually at the beach and there is nothing that can duplicate that experience'.[13] The use of a found environment as the setting for a perfor-

115

59. *Somewhere in the Pacific*

60. *Somewhere in the Pacific*

mance incorporates it into the theatrical work so that it is intended as much for perception as the created objects and events placed in it. In fact Chris Hardman says that people watched the beach perform aided by the Snake Theater.

Snake Theater continued to explore the environmental approach even when they created works which would tour to more traditional indoor venues. Hardman says that most theatre 'uses an actor/prop relationship; an actor moves through a frozen set, now and then manipulating props'. On the other hand, Snake Theater 'masked the actors so they would become props' and they 'animated the props so that they would have as much life as the actors . . . Everything became a kinetic sculpture'.

Large sculptured cacti indicated the setting of *24th Hour Cafe* (1978), which was made to be performed indoors. It was set in the Californian desert at an isolated truckstop cafe with its country-and-western music, truck drivers, and a lonely waitress. The company actually had in mind a specific cafe along a highway in California. The inceptive idea was the feeling of waiting. As in *Somewhere in the Pacific* none of the on-stage performers spoke. Their voices and thoughts as well as narration were provided by slide projections and the live voice of Laura Farabough in the pit, where she also played violin and assisted Lary Graber with the combination of live and recorded music.

The Truck Driver passes through without stopping, leaving miniature metal cut-outs of trucks behind him. The Waitress (Evelyn Lewis) has a cigarette before the arrival of customers, represented by bas-relief sculptures. She tolerates their holding her hand and their stares (indicated by strings from their eyes) as she pours coffee, represented by brown sand. She prepares plates which are cooked by the cactus men, and she serves the inanimate customers as well as the Lizard Man (Christopher Hardman), a stranger who moves on his belly. The Lizard Man flirts with the Waitress, who responds, but the Waitress's lover, the Truck Driver, enters and becomes jealous. He beats up the Waitress and knocks down the customers. The two men, wearing cactus masks, fight over the woman. Later the Truck Driver takes her among the cacti for sex as paintings of people kissing and embracing are shown. The voice of the Waitress says, 'Don't just take me, take me away.' But she is left waiting on customers at the cafe. At the end of the play she is still lonely, still hoping to be taken away, but she is only taken off for sex by the Lizard Man.

Again the narrative is not linear. It combines fragments of thoughts, fantasies, and third-person narration with verbal and visual puns all unified by the music. Images are repeated, each time with a variation providing new information or a different perspective. As in music the variations are understood associationally rather than linearly.

In *Auto* (1979) Snake Theater again combined an actual environment with fictional events. It was performed in a disused gas station. The audience sat with their backs to the main street in Sausalito, California, facing the gas

61. *24th Hour Cafe*

62. *24th Hour Cafe*

63. *24th Hour Cafe*

64. *Auto*, **photo: Ron Blanchette**

65. *Auto*, **photo: Ron Blanchette**

pumps and station building. The story concerns an engineer, his wife and daughter, who have car trouble just as they are setting out on a trip. They pull into a gas station and learn that the car has died from neglect. A funeral ceremony is held and the engineer, because of his anti-auto behaviour, becomes an enemy of the attendants who serve Auto, the power represented by the concept of automatic.

Auto uses the functions of an automatic transmission as a guide to its structure. The play is not divided into scenes but into 'gears' which advance the fragmented story of the engineer and his family. Between the 'gears' are 'shifts' which consist of passages from a manual about automatic transmissions being sung by the female voice of Auto.

The automatic transmission which conveys power from engine to wheels is a metaphor for other kinds of power transfers. There was a time when ordinary people could repair their own cars just as they could harness their horses. That was before the automatic transmission and other self-regulating automatic devices. Now even the engineer who designed it can't repair it. The power has been transferred to the attendants who serve Auto. The engineer is stuck and eventually killed. The play is not anti-automatic, but it does imply a widening gap between the abstract ideas of intellectuals and the concrete reality of the machines for which they are responsible.

The final production of Snake Theater before they became two separate companies was also their first production to tour Europe. *Ride Hard/Die Fast* (1980) is the motto of the Hell's Angels, an organization of motorcycle riders (bikers) whom the play compares with the brotherhood of medieval knights. Like the knights, the Hell's Angels are known for their violence and their independence from the rest of society; they have an identifiable dress and language. The central character is a biker who is run down by an automobile – the mortal enemy of bikers. As he lies between life and death he has

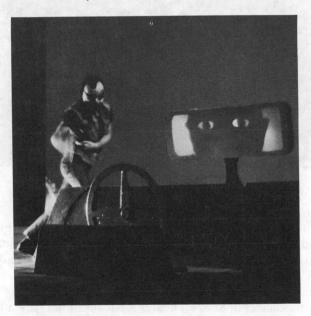

66. *Ride Hard/Die Fast*

a glimpse of 'the wings' which are an emblem of the Nazis as well as the Hell's Angels. The driver of the car is Henry Ford, the inventor of interchangeable parts which historically helped bring an end to certain kinds of individualism. Ford is contrasted with another character, Hitler, who historically saw himself as a romantic hero and thought of his Nazi movement as the last European brotherhood.

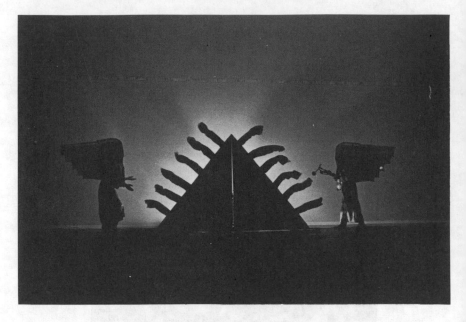

67. *Ride Hard/Die Fast*

As with other Snake Theater productions, the characters and events were abstract and associational rather than literal. Masks, movement, music, mobile props, and dynamic lighting were used to convey mood and character directly. By contrast, realistic drama tends to use language, gestures, and facial expressions to indicate the inner states of characters.

In the performances of Snake Theater the focus of the spectators tended to be on the objects, sounds, and movement themselves rather than on what they indicated or signified. It was somewhat like viewing moving sculpture and listening to music. Even the verbal content was sometimes used for its sound or visual values as much as for its value as discourse. The letter in *Somewhere in the Pacific* as it was revealed on the beach phrase-by-phrase became an important visual element. The words of the letter as sung and chanted by the musicians were of value principally for their sound.

Although there was a fragmentary plot, there was little conventional suspense. The plot did not unravel. Instead, one saw more and more details, connections between images, and formal relationships, giving the work complexity, texture, and richness. Sounds and images seen early in the play, which might have been interesting but apparently isolated and without further significance, became meaningful as the spectators were able to connect them to subsequent images, sounds, words, and movements. One of the pleasures for the spectator was making these connections.

5
New Formalism

Several theatre makers of the 1970s and 1980s are formalists in that their primary concern is form or structure. It becomes the predominant content of their work. These directors are part of one tendency in contemporary art which includes the minimalist painters, makers of happenings, choreographers of post-modern dance, and certain composers of new music.

The association of these theatrical innovators with the formalist vanguard in other arts is not accidental. Each of the theatres discussed in this section is directed by a person who has a background in painting or sculpture, and in one of the companies the leadership is shared with a dancer. Robert Wilson, who began his professional life as a painter, has collaborated with postmodern dance choreographers Lucinda Childs and Andrew de Groat and with composer Philip Glass. The directors of Hellmuth–Reynolds – dancer Suzanne Hellmuth and sculptor Jock Reynolds – have used the music of Steve Reich in their performances. Alan Finneran of Soon 3 worked as both a painter and a sculptor before he began making theatrical productions. And Michael Kirby, the director of the Structuralist Workshop, made some of the early happenings and continues to work as a sculptor.

Typically, vanguard artists have rejected major traditional techniques and materials in order to free their explorations from the limitations of tradition. In 1913 painter Marcel Duchamp rejected the techniques and materials of painting when he attached a bicycle wheel to the top of a wooden stool. The minimalist painters of the 1960s eliminated most painting techniques and all content except the form created by shapes of colour and their compositional relationships. In music Arnold Schönberg dispensed with the traditional diatonic scale and created twelve-tone serial music. John Cage composed

123

music by chance operations thereby avoiding traditional music structures. He experimented with sounds produced by means other than musical instruments, such as the sound of opening and closing a piano keyboard cover. Allan Kaprow, first known as a painter, began making happenings at the end of the 1950s. As with assemblages and environments he considered happenings to be an extension of painting. Any material could be used in happenings except that derived from the arts, and he avoided traditional art techniques and trained artists so as to dissolve the barriers between art and life. Happenings lacked the permanence of traditional visual arts, so they could not be valued as objects or commodities. As a consequence their significance was in perception rather than in the object. Traditional artists embodied in their work specific conceptions which were intended to be conveyed to a spectator. Happenings, on the other hand, were open to a variety of perceptions by various spectators.

As with happenings, minimalist painting, and post-modern dance, the theatre directors included here are predominantly concerned with matters of form and perception. Kaprow's comments on 'formal art' in his book on *Assemblage, Environments & Happenings* apply equally to these theatres.[1] Such art, he says, is primarily intellectual manipulation whereby elements of the work are moved according to strict regulations. Care is taken in choosing the elements so that they do not have such powerful overtones that they take the focus from the form and its manipulation. The impact of the imagery must not be as important as the moves the imagery is put through.

As in happenings and post-modern dances, real-life movements, sounds, objects, and events may be used as material elements in new formalist theatre. When incorporated, however, they are transformed by the context. Following the principle for found art in general, these elements are separated from their real-world efficacy and have value only for perception. It is the same principle by which the environments of Snake Theater's outdoor productions become assimilated into their respective works.

An important difference between happenings and formalist theatre lies in the degree of control exercised by the director and in the circumstances of production. While 'happeners' such as Kaprow prepared scenarios which were discussed with the participants, there were no rehearsals and the performances were not repeated. Had they been presented more than once, each performance would have been quite different in its details. Kaprow also advocated that the happening should take place over several widely-spaced locales because a single performance space would resemble conventional theatre practice. By way of further disassociating with theatrical convention, he proposed that time be discontinuous and that the audience be eliminated entirely. By contrast, the theatre directors of formalist work plan the work in detail and rehearse it until it is precise. A performance continues without a break in time except, perhaps, for an interval. The work is most often presented in a theatre space and always with an audience. There is no limit on the number of performances of a single production.

At the outset all of these theatrical formalists tended to use performers who had not trained as actors. In so doing they paralleled the practice of post-modern dance choreographers who avoided using trained dancers. The choreographers and the theatre directors wanted performers who would move and speak as themselves rather than according to a predetermined style or technique. This applied whether they were required to perform everyday movements or special tasks. The emphasis is on the organization and structure of movement rather than a particular style, virtuosity, or expressiveness. Furthermore, using techniques developed for a traditional style would tend to impose that style on the new work. In genuinely experimental work, it may not be known in advance what skills and techniques will be required. It is better to use performers devoid of technique than to impose an established technique which might limit the exploration. Only after the artists begin to clarify for themselves the unique focus of their work are they inclined to introduce established techniques and use them toward the new purpose.

Robert Wilson

The work of Robert Wilson reflects his training as a painter and architect. His architectonic sketches tend to be the initial concepts for a production. Although he is primarily concerned with visual composition, he is also interested in movement and sound for their structural values. His performance ideas have been further enriched by his work with brain-damaged children, which has led to an interest in creating productions which are perceived in a state of reduced consciousness.

Some of his productions are on a grand operatic scale and resemble large surreal paintings with moving figures and objects. Other work, on a small scale, typically involves only two performers – Wilson and another, sometimes dancer Lucinda Childs. Regardless of scale, his collage-like works incorporate invented material as well as material from the real world. Verbal passages, movement, character ideas, and visual images are transformed into elements that are separate from the spectator's world and without reference to it. The aural and visual images are made to serve the complex formal composition of the production.

In 1969 Wilson formed the Byrd Hoffman School of Byrds to work with people of all backgrounds and capabilities and provide opportunities for them to interact and develop their individual potentials. Although he later used professional performers, in the early productions handicapped people worked on an equal basis with other untrained people he knew or found on the street. He uses physical activity to sensitize the body and thereby expand consciousness.

The performers in *The King of Spain* (1969) were from awareness classes he was conducting which were intended to make the participants more comfortable with their bodies. In the performance Wilson directed the participants to be themselves, to perform the various activities as they themselves would perform them. Wilson has commented that seemingly irrelevant activities, performed in this way, become perceptually important. The activities are intended to be perceived for their own sake rather than serving as clues to inner psychological states.

The productions became longer and longer. *The King of Spain* was incorporated as the second act of *The Life and Times of Sigmund Freud* (1970) which eventually became the first three acts of *Deafman Glance* (1970). In their combined form the performance lasted as long as eight hours. Then Wilson created a prologue for *Deafman Glance* which added another three hours. *The Life and Times of Joseph Stalin* (1973), incorporating all or part of five previous productions, was twelve hours long. The longest production by Wilson was *Overture to Ka Mountain* (1972), created for the Shiraz Festival in Iran. The performance lasted seven days and nights.

One of the reasons his performances are so long is that the events take place in extreme slow motion. At the beginning of *Deafman Glance* there is a tableau of a deaf adolescent black boy, his mother, and two little children (a boy and a girl) who lie on the floor. Nothing moves for half an hour, then very very slowly the mother pours a glass of milk for the little boy, he drinks it, she puts him to bed, slowly and tenderly stabs him, and tucks him under the sheet. Carefully she wipes the knife and repeats the action with the little girl. All the while the older boy watches, unable to move or speak. The action of this first scene takes about one hour.

Slow motion over such an extended period alters drastically the way we perceive the performance. It tends to carry one beyond boredom, beyond the point of being irritated by the slowness, and one tends to adapt by slipping into a mental state that is less acutely conscious than normal. (One of the ingredients of boredom – a feeling of being trapped – is absent because spectators are told they should feel free to go in and out of the auditorium as they wish.) This state of reduced consciousness makes possible the intended mode of perception.

Wilson believes that everyone sees and hears on two different levels. We experience sensations of the world around us on what he calls an 'exterior screen'. But we also become aware of things on an 'interior screen' – dreams and daydreams for instance. Blind people only 'see' things on an interior visual screen and deaf people can only 'hear' sounds on an interior audial screen. Wilson found that in his long performances the spectator's interior-exterior audial–visual screens become one. Interior and exterior images mingle so that they are indistinguishable. Wilson says that people sometimes 'see' things on stage that are not actually there.[2]

The development of this concept resulted from his work with two adolescent boys – Raymond Andrews, the deaf mute who played the title role in *Deafman Glance,* and Christopher Knowles, the autistic fourteen-year-old who became Wilson's collaborator on several productions. Both boys were partially cut off from the exterior world – Andrews as a result of being unable to hear or speak, and Knowles because of brain damage which caused him to be absorbed in fantasy. They were 'less conscious' than other people, more closed off from the objective world, more absorbed with inner images than with external reality. They were in a kind of trance. Both of them, Wilson came to realize, had highly developed interior screens. He became interested in discovering how they structured their perceptions in order to understand what their worlds were like. Then, with their help, Wilson created productions that attempted to deal with reality in similar ways.

Wilson and the other members of the workshop imitated Andrews's sounds and movements in order to discover the way the eleven-year-old thought and communicated. They believed that his way of perceiving the world was as valid as theirs and they wanted to understand it. In the course of workshops for *Deafman Glance* they discovered that repetition of simple movements was a means of tuning to interior screens, a practice used by people in other cultures to enter a trance.

Christopher Knowles, when he began working with Wilson, used words but he did not use them for the usual aim of discourse. Instead, he seemed to be using words as sounds, as music, and sometimes for the visual patterns they would form then typed on paper. Knowles led workshops in which the group imitated his sounds, and his work formed the basis for the use of language in *A Letter for Queen Victoria* (1974). He also was responsible for some of the language used in the five-hour opera *Einstein on the Beach* (1976).

Einstein on the Beach was created by Wilson in collaboration with com-poser Philip Glass and choreographers Andrew de Groat and Lucinda Childs, who design geometric patterns in controlled space. The production incorporates techniques of repetition, extreme slow motion as well as fast repetitive dance movements, and non-discursive use of language. As in Wilson's other works there is no traditional dramatic narrative, but a visual and aural stream of images. The opera has a mathematical structure of nine scenes. There are three dominant visual images, each appearing in every third scene so that each is used three times. The images are (1) a train and a building, (2) a courtroom and a bed, (3) a field with a spaceship. Each act is preceded and followed by a musical 'Knee Play' (that is, a joint) which serves as prelude, interlude, or postlude.

Most of the performers are dressed like Einstein in shirt, baggy pants, and suspenders. The solo violinist, made-up like the elderly Einstein, looks on from his detached position in the orchestra pit. In the first scene a ten-year-old boy, suggesting Einstein as a child, looks down from a bridge as a nine-teenth-century steam locomotive moves onto the stage so slowly that its movement is imperceptible. The slow-moving train is accompanied by the fast movement of several performers who repeat the same gestures and steps for the entire thirty-minute scene. Lucinda Childs skip-steps forward and backward on three diagonals while the gestures of another performer

68. *Einstein on the Beach*

suggest the writing of mathematical equations. When the train appears again (scene 4) it is the last car of a night train slowly moving on a diagonal away from the audience. In its third appearance (scene 7) it has been transformed into a brick building which echoes the lines and perspective of the train.

In the courtroom scenes (2, 5, and 8) a large clock without hands is eclipsed by a black disc moving imperceptibly slowly. In the first courtroom scene a platform in the foreground is the abstracted form of a bed. When the courtroom appears again half of the stage is transformed into a prison.

Inside the play's structure of recurring dominant images is a loose association of images about the life and times of Einstein and after. The train image of the first scene suggests the age of steam when Einstein was a boy dreaming of aeroplanes. In the last scene – the interior of a space ship with lights flashing in complex patterns – we have reached the nuclear age of space travel exemplifying the theories of Einstein. In between are trials and prison. Everything is unified and dominated by the architectural grandeur of the settings and the precise, repetitious, carefully constructed music of Philip Glass.

Philip Glass wrote the music for *Einstein on the Beach* responding directly to a series of Wilson's drawings. (These architectonic sketches were Wilson's inceptive idea for the opera and eventually they were the basis for the set designs.) The music, which is sung or played continuously throughout

69. *Einstein on the Beach*

70. *Einstein on the Beach*

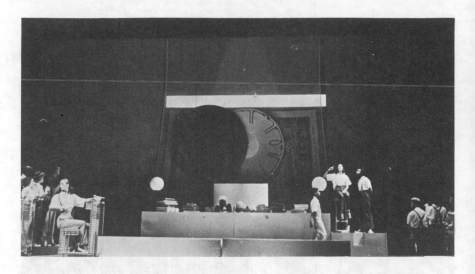

71.　*Einstein on the Beach*

72.　*Einstein on the Beach*

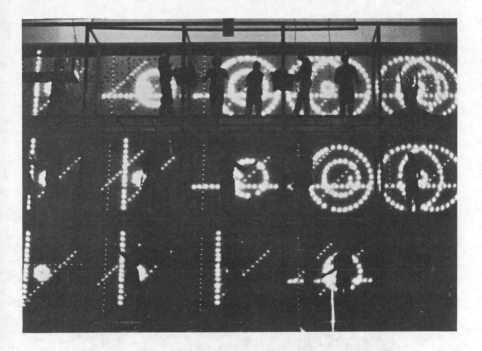

73. *Einstein on the Beach*

the performance, is as precisely constructed as the visual elements. For each of the recurring visual themes there is a musical theme. Sometimes the music is performed by an amplified ensemble of keyboards, winds, and violin; at other times amplified singers perform alone; and sometimes the ensemble and singers perform at once. The only words sung are the numbers one through eight and the sol-fa syllables – do, re, mi, and so forth. Not only are the numbers appropriate to the theme of Einstein, they represent the rhythmic structure (it is the way beats are counted). The sol-fa syllables represent the pitch structure (normally they are used to sing the scale). So, the text is descriptive of the music itself.

The usual predominance in Western music of melody and harmony over rhythm is reversed in the music of Glass. It is one of the means of making the structure audible. But there are other techniques which serve to keep structure and process in focus. He uses cyclic structures and an additive process. A musical phrase is repeated over and over, then it is changed slightly and repeated over and over again, and so forth. One is able to perceive the process. The form, created from structure and process, is the dominant content of the music as well as the opera as a whole.

The spoken passages, like the music, are used for their aural rather than their discursive value. Some of them by Christopher Knowles are disjointed and make use of recurring phrases. Others are non-dramatic, often banal conversational passages created by the performers through improvisation

74. *I Was Sitting on My Patio*

and writing. In the performance they are repeated over and over with identical inflection so that they lose their initial meanings and, like the musical phrases, become structured sound.

The play incorporates Wilson's free mental associations about the fourth dimension relating time and space as well as the technological world inspired by Einstein. But the play is also self-reflexive. It is this same technology which made the physical production of the play impossible with its complicated and expensive electronics and musical amplification systems designed and built specifically for this production. At the core of the work is a mathematical structure. Not only do the dominant images recur on a mathematical schedule, but the choreography of Andrew de Groat and especially the music of Philip Glass are precisely constructed on numerical systems. Glass says that the singers do everything by numbers, sometimes counting two or three things at once – the numbers they are singing, the measures, and the speed of a movement such as bringing a finger to the upper lip on a count of thirty-two.

Einstein on the Beach is the most elaborate production by Wilson to date. It cost approximately one million dollars to tour the opera houses of Europe

75. *I Was Sitting on My Patio*

before its two final performances at the Metropolitan Opera House in New York. By contrast his production the following year was comparatively simple and uncomplicated, although it used some of the same technology and had the same formalist approach. Robert Wilson and Lucinda Childs were the only performers in *I Was Sitting on My Patio/This Guy Appeared I Thought/I Was Hallucinating* (1977).[3]

The play consists of two identical forty-minute monologues made up of more than one hundred story fragments. The title is one of these fragments. Wilson, alone on stage, gives the first monologue and then Childs, also alone, speaks the second monologue which contains the same fragments. They speak in a quiet conversational tone and are amplified by wireless microphones worn by the performers. It is as if we were hearing their minds directly, their jumbled thinking, flitting from one banality to another in an a-logical stream-of-consciousness manner. Wilson says that the language was written more as 'a reflection of the way we think than of the way we normally speak'. He compares it to flipping from channel to channel on a television set. Sometimes when he writes he has a television playing at low volume and incorporates phrases that he hears.[4]

The setting is a simple architectural design – three large windows which become three large bookcases, a bench-like metal bed, a glass shelf with a wine glass, and a telephone on a small table. As a performer speaks he or she moves naturally around the stage. But the movement does not relate to what is being said, it is abstract motion in space, sometimes deliberately contra-dicting what is implied by the words.

In her unpublished notes, Lucinda Childs says her work on the production involved the same kind of exploration as her earlier post-modern dance explorations as a member of the Judson Dance Theatre. The Judson work expanded the vocabulary of dance so as to include movement from everyday life. Also, instead of putting images, words, and action together so as to make sense, they isolated them and pulled them apart, playing one element against another. She says it is the spectator's job 'to make sense out of what he sees and to decide if it's chaos or order, formed or formless, or if that matters'.

Although the phrases and movement have the natural quality of everyday banalities, they are distanced by the microphone and by the fact that words and movement are disassociated. Each performer has decided on his or her own movements. So, there are interesting echoes and contrasts between the concrete image of Childs in front of us and the remembered image of what Wilson did on a particular phrase.

In *I Was Sitting on My Patio* Wilson has found another means of creating harmony and opposition between our interior and exterior screens, between memory and that being perceived at the moment. As in all of his other work, he is interested not only in form but in exploring the ways people perceive and how perception can be altered.

Suzanne Hellmuth and Jock Reynolds

The theatre work created by dancer Suzanne Hellmuth and sculptor Jock Reynolds uses images which derive from their observations in the real world. These images are used as formal elements in a moving composition. Like the other theatrical formalists, their work keeps the spectator's focus on the surface, on a form both visual and aural, not on what may be implied or on an underlying psychology. They carefully avoid overt sociological or political meaning. Because they do not create a fictional time–place context and there are no characters, even though there are performers, there is no plot suspense to focus the audience on an evolving future. Instead the spectator relates to the form.

As with the work of Wilson, one tends to respond to the productions of Hellmuth–Reynolds from a state of reduced consciousness. This results from some of the same techniques used by Wilson – repetitive movements, slow motion, and the extensive use of new music, especially the additive pro-cess music of Steve Reich. Also like Wilson's, their work is predominantly visual – in fact, in their large-scale productions they use no words at all. The way in which they develop a production, however, is very different.

Hellmuth and Reynolds base their productions on personal observations, experiences, and research undertaken in specific places in San Francisco where they live. This has been the approach of Reynolds since the early

1970s when he created sculptures using material and live animals from the Californian farm where he then lived. While on the farm he began raising and slaughtering animals for food, and he did a performance with the heads of two pigs he had raised and butchered.

This practice of extracting performances from his current experience continued when he began working with Suzanne Hellmuth, whose background had been in dance. Reynolds's mother was dying of cancer during this period and before her death in 1974 he had spent much time visiting her in the hospital. Suzanne Hellmuth had also had experiences with hospitals – her brother died after being hit by a drunken driver and she had been hospitalized for illnesses of her own. Having decided to make a production on the subject they began practical research. A hospital in San Francisco permitted them to observe most activities and they talked with patients and employees. *Hospital* (1977), their first major work together, combined the theatrical sculpture focus of Reynolds with the dance interests of Hellmuth.

The work is without narrative. Instead it is made up of sounds, images, props, and tasks abstracted from those Hellmuth and Reynolds had discovered during their hospital research. These elements were scored much as if they were different musical instruments and notes in a musical composition. While the audience recognizes many of the tasks as the usual hospital activities of doctors, nurses, patients, and janitors, they are not performed in a realistic fashion. Instead they are abstracted, becoming dance-like exaggerations, repetitions, or slowed action, accompanied by the sounds of squeaking shoes, whistling tea kettles, bells, plates on meal-trays, and the music of Steve Reich.

Hospital was presented in San Francisco at the Magic Theatre in an area of about 650 square metres. Seating was constructed along one wall. The remaining space, used for the performance, is divided into five planes, each extending thirty metres from the audience's extreme left to extreme right. Often there is simultaneous movement in several of these. In the plane closest to the audience a row of three hospital rooms is indicated by rectangles on the floor. Behind the rooms is a hallway, then a movable curtain, a large corridor, a metal cyclone fence, and another hallway and wall with five doors.

For the 'Solarium' scene the curtain is closed and the only movement consists of shadows of hospital images – a nurse (Suzanne Hellmuth) carrying pillows, a patient in a wheelchair. In the 'Slow Walk' scene several actions are performed simultaneously at different tempos. A nurse in the near hallway walks in slow motion. In the large corridor three janitors collect buckets, and two nurses walk very slowly, gently pitching and yawing like a sailboat. In the distant hallway two nurses walk in slow motion switching on the overhead lights. Two doctors with two-metre-long satchels slowly walk through the hallways. A man and two children walk in normal tempo to visit a woman patient; when they arrive they sit and talk quietly.

In another scene, a nurse in each of the hospital rooms spins like a whirling

76. *Hospital*, **photo: Bill Hellmuth**

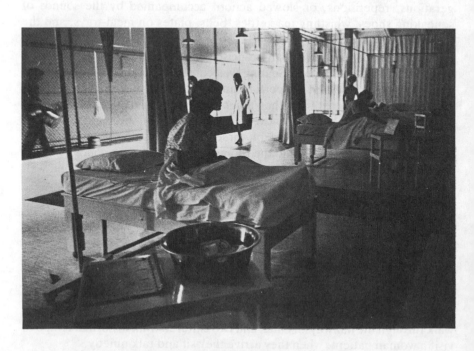

77. *Hospital*, **photo: Jock Reynolds**

78. *Hospital*, **photo: Bill Hellmuth**

dervish as other nurses pass in the hallway. In the 'Surgeons' Dance' thirteen performers appear by ones, twos, and small groups until all are in place. Their dance consists of a choreographed series of gestures using only their eyes and hands.

'Accumulation/Treatment' uses the entire space. Two janitors in the distant hallway place large red keys on the far wall and set them swinging as nurses perform waiting movements – shifting weight, putting hands in and out of pockets. Patients lie on the floor on bed-sized rectangles and a nurse places a calibrated white stick across the body of each. At the nurses' station two nurses pivot in slow motion as they move soundless bells. A nurse walks through the corridor pushing giant white wheels. At the very end a hospital technician (Jock Reynolds) wheels a rack of laboratory animals through the corridor.

Unlike those theatres advocating social change that might study a hospital in order to present a socio-political analysis, for Hellmuth and Reynolds *Hospital* was a means of making their hospital experience more objective by focusing on the perceptual aspects of their experience – the visual and aural aspects – rather than on their subjective reaction of repugnance and loss.

In preparation for *Navigation* (1979) Hellmuth and Reynolds explored two different locales – San Francisco Bay with its ships and other nautical elements, and the large well-equipped theatre where the production was to be presented. Observing the Bay they were greatly affected by the gigantic scale of the bands of land, water, and sky, by the awesomeness of large ships

79. *Hospital*, **photo: Bill Hellmuth**

passing silently or rocking at anchor, by the changes in light as the day passes, by the sense of balancing on a rolling deck, and by the quietness, and the sounds. As they worked in the theatre building they were struck by its monumental scale, its austere functionality, the activities of technicians and maintenance workers. They became aware of the similarities between theatres and ships, especially the beauty of functional structure. The relationship was reinforced as they looked through photo archives of ships, seeing sailors dwarfed by the rigging and sails with which they worked.

The performance of *Navigation* uses the mechanisms of the theatre in the same undisguised manner as those of a ship. The rigging, the flats, workshop doors, paint racks, the unpainted concrete walls, are all used as visual elements. The mechanism of the theatre is activated by the crew and used by the performers in an analogous way to crews and passengers aboard ships.

The slow motion of the performance suggests the rhythm of ships at sea responding to the waves, wind, and currents. Bands of flats, stretching across the entire twenty-metre stage, raise and lower and swing slowly from side to side like the horizon line seen from the prow of a ship. All of the images are abstract rather than literal. Performers coil ropes which they pull from holes in the floor, and they sway as if to maintain balance. A large door opens at the rear of the stage and the image seen there suggests a sailboat passing in the distance. There are other nautical suggestions – large grids like nets, a wall which sways from side to side, and sailors with signalling devices.

80. *Navigation*

81. *Navigation*

Although the objects and movement on stage suggest ships, water, and sky, there is no realistic illusion. With the help of the music of David Behrman's 'On the Other Ocean' with its electronic synthesizer, flute, and oboe, the spectators are made to focus on the formal aspects of the work. As

82. *Navigation*

in *Hospital* Suzanne Hellmuth and Jock Reynolds have transformed their experience of an environment into perceptible form.

Alan Finneran
Soon 3

The 'performance landscapes' of Alan Finneran began as extensions of the mobile painting and sculpture with which he was experimenting in the mid-1960s. The performances project a technological landscape of manufactured and precisely-constructed abstract objects which serves as an environment for the tasks of performers. Although they do not present a coherent illusion of a fictional world, in the most recent work the spectator's perception of the objects and performed tasks is 'coloured' by music, lighting, film and slide projections, repetition, language with the economy of poetry, and a fragmentary narrative.

Finneran first added performers to his kinetic sculptures in 1967. In 1972, when he moved from Boston to San Francisco and formed Soon 3, he began construction of a 'theatre machine' consisting of elaborate moving sculptures with rotating projection screens on which films and slides were projected. When *The Desire Circus* (1975) was presented at the San Francisco Museum of Modern Art it incorporated twelve performers who were little more than compositional elements.

83. *Black Water Echo*

Beginning in 1977 with the first 'task activated landscape', the visual effects were achieved without the 'theatre machine' but continued the use of projections and the hard-edge manufactured look. The landscape of *Black Water Echo* is defined by a square of black plastic. Neatly arranged at the sides of the square are all of the objects to be used in the performance – doughnut-shaped fluorescent lights, small plexiglass houses with removable roofs, plastic tubes. These objects are manipulated by a Man and a Woman who carry out their tasks without enacting characters or emotions. The manipulations create a new element. The environment is given a past and a future. At the beginning of the performance the landscape is pristine, but by the end it is cluttered with debris comprising a history of the tasks performed there. The objects and projections are not merely an environment, they are as important as the non-speaking Man and Woman. There is a symbiotic relationship between the two elements. Changes made in the landscape by the performers cause changes in the actions of the performers.

In Finneran's works there is no pre-existing concept from which the performance grows, no idea to be investigated or illustrated. Instead, like an abstract painter, he makes intuitive decisions about the objects, colours, performers, tasks, and other elements which will comprise the production. This intuitive approach is more like that of Robert Wilson than that of Hellmuth–Reynolds, which begins with observation and research.

His next production, *A Wall in Venice/3 Women/Wet Shadows* (1978),

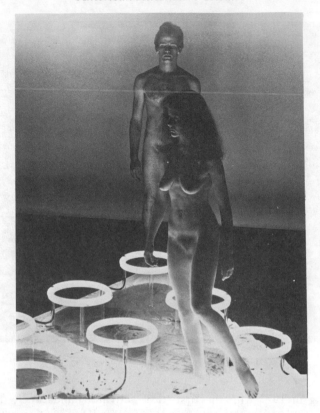

84. *Black Water Echo*, **photo: Alan Finneran**

85. *Black Water Echo*

hints at a fictional illusion. For the first time the figures are named, the apparent place of the action is identified, and there is a fragmentary recorded narrative. These new elements, however, are no more important than the others. They are used more as a means of 'colouring' the events than of causing the spectators to acknowledge a fictional world.

At the beginning a recorded voice presents an open narrative intentionally incomplete. It begins,

> That evening I was rowing close to shore when I saw her.
> She was swimming alone in the cold water.
> She came close to my boat.
> She pretended not to notice me.
>
> . . .

We also learn that each of the three women is named Scarlet and that two of them live in a blue house on the canal. But there is no relationship between the narrative and the tasks of the performers unless the spectator contrives one. A red dress casts a shadow on the floor. One of the women in red (Candace Loheed) stands white dowels on end outlining the shadow, and another woman (Bean Finneran) also in red pulls a red pyramid on wheels through the dowels knocking them down.

86. *A Wall in Venice/3 Women/Wet Shadows*

87. *A Wall in Venice*

The spectators are made to focus on the actual objects and tasks in the present moment rather than being seduced into a psychic involvement with fictional time, place, and characters. They relate to the work of Soon 3 much as they would to sculpture in a gallery – aware of the illusion created but seeing it as an object in the present. This way of relating to the work is enhanced by showing the means used to create the illusion. In one segment of *A Wall in Venice* a woman places a tiny white house on the floor. On a larger house-shaped screen behind the tiny house a photographic seascape is projected, and the sounds of seagulls and water are heard. She places small potted palm

88.   *A Wall in Venice*

trees beside the tiny house and turns on an electric fan which makes them
sway as if the wind were blowing. She sets up a movie projector which projects on the front of the tiny house a film of the second woman so that she
appears to be standing in front of her house. A slide of the second woman is
projected life-size on the front of the larger house, and the live second
woman cuts a slit in it from behind and 'materializes'. She then goes to the
tiny house and sets it on fire. Throughout the segment we are able to observe
both the illusion and the means by which it is being created.

   Tropical Proxy (1979) incorporates snatches of live dialogue, but these do
not serve any of the usual purposes. Here the dialogue is not used to reveal
character relationships, psychological states, or plot exposition. Instead, as
with Finneran's use of music, it affects our perception of the visual events
and, like his narrative fragments, serves to pique our curiosity.

B: Remember the last time this happened?
N: Yeah, I remember – nothing happened.

A projected sign says, 'mombasa kenya 1970'. Four white women sit on high stools facing the audience, each with a live black rabbit on her lap. Again there are several references to water. A clear plastic tank of water is prominent throughout, sometimes a sailboat floats on it, and there is a narrative fragment about a fire at sea. Again there are tasks which alter the stage environment. A concrete-block house is erected on one side of the stage, a room is painted blue on the other. Miniature buildings are set up near the tank of water and a tiny seaport takes shape.

The next Soon 3 work, *The Man in the Nile at Night* (1980), does not use dialogue, but the foreign woman's voice on tape is interrogating someone who apparently replies with gestures.

Was it at night?
Was it?
Were you in the water with him?
. . .
Which stocking did you take off first?
Please take that one off now.
Thank you. Now please drop the stocking onto the floor.

There is a mystery. The two live performers open suitcases, change clothes, and put on black wigs. A projection says, 'Cairo 1953'. One of the women removes a blue stocking from a room by tying a string to it and pulling it through a yellow door. A rod is pushed through a hole in a miniature yellow door and it 'bleeds' blue dye into a plexiglass tank of water. Several times projections of a man appear. Finally the two women burn the screen on which his image is projected. Actions on stage echo in an abstract way verbal descriptions, but the fragments of the story intentionally do not add up to a coherent whole. The work creates a strong focus not only because of the dynamic, animated, visible and audible compositions, but because it is so intriguing and mysterious that the spectator is seduced into projecting subjective interpretations upon the events. The results are rich, both perceptually and conceptually.

The Man in the Nile at Night and *A Wall in Venice* toured Italy in 1980. In the following year a new work was created during a three-months' residency at Theater am Turm, the experimental theatre centre in Frankfurt-am-Main. *Renaissance Radar* is described as a 'performance landscape' and uses some elements similar to those of other productions – mobile sculptural objects, three women who are sometimes in red, film and slide projections, pre-recorded narrative fragments, and music. However, the production is different from Finneran's previous performance landscapes in several ways.

Because the scale of *Renaissance Radar* is much larger than other recent

89. *Tropical Proxy***, photo: Ron Blanchette**

90. *The Man in the Nile at Night*

work, it suggests his productions of the mid-1970s which used the 'theatre machine'. The most elaborate mechanical device is a giant remote-controlled projection screen in the shape of a head on which is projected a sound film close-up of one of the performers speaking.

For the first time in Finneran's work, two places rather than one are indicated by projected captions alternating between 'Roma 1474' and 'California 1980'. However, as in previous Soon 3 productions, an indicated place serves only to colour the events that occur, it does not become an illusory setting for action. The action consists of tasks in the present on a manufactured landscape.

Renaissance Radar was the first Soon 3 production to use music composed especially for it. Working closely with Finneran, composer Bob Davis created a continuous score which functions somewhat like a motion picture sound-track. Using conventional instruments, synthesizer, and concrete sounds combined and electronically altered, this pre-recorded score suggests both the renaissance and San Francisco New Wave.

Another innovation is the conscious use of what Finneran refers to as a 'compositional theme' – the 'idea of murder and violence as product, especially the illusionary product of the California movie industry'. Three women – a Victim, a Killer, and an Accomplice – perform three murders accomplished with the use of modern technology. In the first murder the nude Victim is wired with twelve explosive devices such as those used in motion pictures to create the illusion of a person being shot. In the second, an imaginary device constructed of plexiglass, hoses and knives are used to stab projected images of the Victim. Finally, the Victim is enclosed in a plexiglass tank which is then filled with water while she breathes with the aid of an aqua-lung. These murders serve as the chief structural element of the production, but they do not comprise a conventional plot. They are experienced more as demonstrations by performers who do not seem to enact characters or emotions. Finneran suggests that the murders can also be seen as technical demonstrations of tricks used in Hollywood movies to create the illusion of violence. As in other Soon 3 productions the means used to create illusion are considered as important as the illusion itself, and the spectator is intended to be aware of both.

Alan Finneran is highly skilled in combining sound and visual elements in such a way that they lose their neutrality and are transformed into an environment charged with expectation. It is not the suspense of fiction, as the spectator focuses on the present time and place, but when a task is initiated there is a kind of suspense until it is completed. There is a matrix – a physical space and pattern of movement which, like any formal structure whether a sonnet or a building under construction, is in suspense until completed. There is also interest in the narrative and dialogue fragments which, like a puzzle, we may attempt to fit together with the other parts. But the narrative does not provide the cause-and-effect unity of fictional dramatic action. Instead, the work is unified by the cause-and-effect relationship of the tasks which are mutated by the changes such tasks make in the actual stage space; and the shapes, colours, and recognizable objects are related through repetition, counterpoint, transformation, and visual echoes.

Michael Kirby
The Structuralist Workshop

In conventional realistic theatre the artists attempt to hide structure. If the audience becomes conscious of the structural mechanism, it will detract from the apparent life passing before them. Structure in such works is a means of creating suspense which keeps the audience absorbed in the fictional world. Technique hides technique. In the structuralist works of Michael Kirby, however, the end *is* structure and how it is perceived.

In his 'Manifesto of Structuralism' (1975) and in a subsequent article on structural analysis and theory (1976)[5] Kirby outlines the tenets of his theatre. He uses 'structure' to refer to 'the way the parts of a work relate to each other, how they "fit together" in the mind to form a particular configuration'. He is concerned with formal (rather than semantic) structures. While the structural principles of painting and sculpture can be applied to performance, in performance there is also the dimension of time which, according to Kirby, can be seen as 'a sequence of present moments, each of which moves away to become part of the past'. It is expectancy and memory that provide the structural relationship between these moments. While it is typical for structure to dominate in music and dance when words and mimetic action are not used, in theatre performances which use a semantic element, meaning tends to take over. Kirby's objective is to use words, real objects, and fragments of realistic scenes to create performances in which structure dominates.

'Structuralism is primarily mental or intellectual,' says Kirby. 'The mind works as it attempts to understand arrangements and interrelationships.'[6] The spectator may consciously recognize structure in Kirby's plays, may have a heightened awareness of its presence, or may merely be aware of reflections, echoes, premonitions, answers, frustrations, or fulfilments. Whether working as a sculptor, a maker of happenings, or a playwright and theatre director, Michael Kirby consistently creates works in which structure dominates. A typical sculpture consists of photographs taken from various perspectives according to a precise system and then mounted in a geometrical configuration reflecting the system.

In a 1966 happening, *Room 706,* he used acting for the first time as distinct from tasks assigned to participants. Principally the work consisted of an impromptu discussion of plans for the performance. The discussion was presented three times: (1) on audio tape, (2) on film, and (3) in a live performance using a script transcribed from the tape recording. The concept of three was echoed in the physical arrangements for the performance, an equilateral triangle with the audience seated on three sides. At each corner of the triangle was a table with a tape recorder, and in the centre three rectangular tables were arranged to form a triangle. First the tape recording of the discussion is heard with one voice coming from each corner. Then the film is projected from the centre tables to a screen at each corner. Later the same scene is acted live by the three men in the original discussion.

In his plays, the principle means used to put structure into the foreground is a systematized repetition of related movements, speeches, sounds, objects, and images presented verbally or visually. There is always the hint of a narrative which creates a mystery, but the story is never complete. For *Revolutionary Dance* he wrote seven short scenes consisting of basic movements and speeches by people who seem to be involved in civil war activities in an unnamed country. The scenes were then put together in a certain order, but they could have gone in any order. It was the structural repetitions that were important. In *Eight People* there were twenty-five short scenes suggesting a story of love and espionage. There were echoes of dialogue phrases; recurring gestures such as ripping up a letter, tearing open a box of cookies, tearing up a manuscript; repetition of spacial and movement patterns – in three scenes a woman stands in the centre of a triangle formed by three other people and turns to each one as they speak. There were reappearing objects such as umbrellas, rakes, tape recorders and suitcases. Sounds were repeated such as raking leaves, and in every third scene there was the sound of a telephone being dialled and ringing.

In *Photoanalysis* (1976) three projection screens face the audience. In front of the centre screen is a lectern and a male lecturer. In front of each side screen is a woman with a chair or a stool. These three figures take regular turns speaking – first the man, then the woman on the left, then the woman on the right. As each speaks, a series of three photographic slides is projected on the screen behind that person. Each person speaks ten times, so thirty slides are shown on each screen.

The lecturer uses the slides on his screen to illustrate his talk on photoanalysis which he considers the newest science. By means of such analysis, he says, we can discover the subjective meanings of photographs. The lecture is repetitious, sometimes pointing out the obvious and at other times drawing unfounded conclusions. It is Kirby's parody of subjective criticism masking as objective science. The two women, when they speak, do not refer to the projections. Instead, each tells a story of a strange incident in her life.

The woman on the left is a widow whose husband Carl drowned in a stream under strange circumstances. However, there are suggestions that he might not be dead. She found one of his shirts wringing wet in the house. A friend found one of Carl's gloves. The projections seem to illustrate various places and objects mentioned in the story. The house where she lived with Carl, a nearby bridge, a large country house, playing cards seen on a table and later in a dry creek bed, a hand holding a glass with ice cubes, a graveyard, and so forth. The same man and woman appear in many of the slides. Similar but not identical photographs of the same subjects are shown in a dif-

91. *Photoanalysis*

ferent order on the screens behind the other two performers when they speak. The slides shown on the right screen are in the reverse order to those on the left.

When the woman on the right speaks, incidents in her story remind us of moments in the story of the woman on the left. She tells of visiting a friend called Amy in her San Francisco house. Strange things were seen there – for example, a man's shirt although no man seemed to live there. Amy mentioned a friend named Carlos. They were involved in some sort of covert political group, perhaps having to do with terrorism. Later Carlos was assassinated.

During the play one speculates on the possibility of Carl and Carlos being the same person. The lives of the two women might be intertwined without them knowing it. This is reinforced by the fact that the same places are shown in the projections which illustrate the two stories. Is there a connection between them? Yes, but it is only structural. Our suspicions are never answered. There is merely a web of anticipations and memories created by echoes of visual images and narrative fragments. The lecturer does not acknowledge the presence of the women and is unaware of the significance of his illustrative photographs to their lives. To him they are simply documents for analysis.

The acting area for *Double Gothic* (1978) is shaped like a large box about six metres square. The audience is divided in half and sits on opposite sides of the box looking into it. The two halves cannot see each other because six

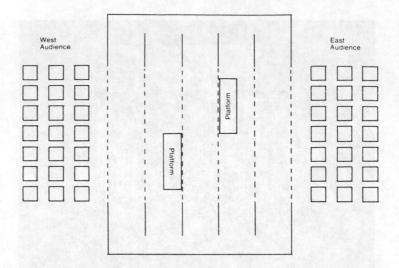

92. **Acting area,** *Double Gothic*, **photo:** *Theatre Design & Technology*

black scrims are hung inside the box parallel to the rows of seats. These form five corridors each 1.2 metres wide. In two corridors are platforms which serve as beds. Usually only one corridor is lit at a time.

Two incomplete stories reminiscent of gothic novels are presented in alternating scenes. A scene from story A is played in the outside East corridor. Then the first scene from story B is performed in the outside West corridor. Each subsequent scene is presented one corridor further into the box. The third scene in each story occurs in the centre corridor. Then the two stories pass each other.

In story A a young woman in the near corridor puts down a suitcase. A passing car is heard, she waves but the car does not stop. She sits on the suitcase and examines one of her shoes which is broken. Someone unseen by the spectators has come near and the young woman smiles and says, 'Hello, I had an accident.' Lights go out and come up on story B in the far corridor. A young woman puts down a suitcase and opens an umbrella. In the distance a howling dog is heard. She seems to get something in her eye and examines it. Apparently someone has approached, and she speaks: 'It's not raining, is it?' The lights go out and come up again on the woman with the broken shoe for another short scene, then back to the woman with the umbrella, and so forth, alternating throughout the play. The woman with the broken shoe is met by another woman – a deaf mute with an arm in a sling who carries a lantern and leads her to a large house where they meet an older woman in a wheelchair. When the phone rings, the deaf mute mysteriously answers it. The young woman undresses for bed and discovers a snake in the bed. Putting on a glove, the young woman grabs the snake. The woman in the wheelchair accuses the deaf mute of playing a joke. In the night the deaf mute awakens the young woman and tells her she must leave, it isn't safe

93. *Double Gothic*, **photo: Michael Kirby**

here. Alone again the young woman picks up a lamp, begins exploring the corridors and then disappears.

In the second story, the young woman arrives by train and is met by a blind woman with a cane who leads her to a sanatorium run by a woman doctor. It seems the blind woman can see as she points to the house with her cane. When the young woman is getting ready for bed the doctor discovers a lily in the room, which is dangerous because it uses oxygen. The doctor accuses her blind associate of putting it there. In the night the blind woman awakens the young woman and tells her she must leave. The dialogue is the same as in the first story. She takes a candelabra, explores the corridors, and disappears.

In the beginning of the play, the performance of one story is close to each audience and the other is barely visible through five scrims. As it progresses, the close story recedes and the distant one comes nearer; eventually they pass through each other. This change takes place systematically, providing a spacial structure much as the alternating of scenes makes for a time structure. Once the audience realizes that the two stories are similar, there are many memory connections made across time, and these serve as structural mechanisms 'holding together' units of time. The spectator also begins to anticipate parallel events and images which relate time; and when they occur, there is a sense of structure being fulfilled. These anticipations and memories, sensitized by echoes, concordances, repetitions and parallels, make up a web of relationships that are purely formal. As Kirby points out, no new information is produced when the connections are made.

In all of Michael Kirby's plays there are motifs of mystery – apparent political intrigues, assassinations, possible suicides, implied terrorist activities, gothic tales. No solution is presented to the mysteries – in fact the questions are never fully formulated. The real intrigue is the schematic structure which one attempts to grasp. The fulfilment is a fulfilment of form as we experience a structure being completed much as we would in a musical composition.

All of the new formalists, like Kirby, use narrative elements in their work, but like the other elements they are primarily compositional. The narrative is open, fragmentary, too many questions are left unanswered for there to be a specific narrative meaning. The audience may project their own interpretations upon the fragments, but such interpretations are subjective. The form is the content.

6
Self as Content

The creators of some alternative performances are themselves the primary focus of their work. Some aspect of self becomes the principal content of their productions as well as the chief material from which the productions are made. In some instances the content is the artists' own cognitive and perceptual processes, in others it is autobiographical incidents from their lives, in still others they present themselves on stage as themselves but sometimes in such a way that it is not clear what is actual and what is illusion.

In a fundamental way all alternative theatre puts the performer more in focus than does conventional realistic theatre. Often the performer is seen through the character. However, in some productions of the Living Theatre, notably *Paradise Now,* the performers played themselves in so far as that is possible while being observed by spectators, attempting to engage them, and speaking some predetermined lines. In *Dionysus in 69* the Performance Group worked with the duality of performer and character. Sometimes actors were called by their names, at other times by the names of the characters. Performer and character were indistinguishable. In the performances of Soon 3 the performers simply carry out tasks, although they are done in a prescribed manner and more precisely than if they were not performing.

Similarly, all performances necessarily draw upon the experience and imaginings of the artists. However, some groups use their experience more literally in their performances. One of the plays of Lilith – A Women's Theatre is about the family of one of the performers and is set in the family pizzeria. The first productions of the Gay Theatre Collective in San Francisco and Spiderwoman Theatre Workshop in New York were developed around the personal stories of their members.

Many of the performances by visual artists use the self as content. The objective of Allan Kaprow and others to break down the barriers between life and art were partly achieved by those practising body art. Such work also attempted to shed the concept of the work of art as an object of commercial value. Admission was sometimes charged, however, and documentary photographs, films, and video tapes have become saleable items.

The body art of Californian artist Chris Burden makes performance and actuality coincide. His works from 1971 until about 1975 involved physical risk which tended to eradicate the performance sensibility of the artist who responded to the actual circumstances of the performance. In *Shoot* he arranged for a friend to shoot him in the arm. *Deadman* consisted of Burden lying under a tarpaulin on a Los Angeles street. He has had himself chained to the floor between bare electrical wires and buckets of water, which if kicked over would have electrocuted him. He has had pins stuck into his stomach, has crawled on broken glass, and has had himself imprisoned in a locker for five days.

More in the spirit of fun, but still focused on the bodies of the performers, are the presentations of the Kipper Kids in Los Angeles. Harry Kipper and Harry Kipper wear only jock straps during their scatological performances. They drink beer or whisky, mumble to each other and the audience, sing, belch, fart, and generally make a grotesque mess as they smear themselves and each other with food, mustard, and paint. The audience laughs nervously as they are intimidated with vulgarities and threatened by flying food. However, the performance shifts to the edge of brutality when, in a one-man boxing match, one of the Harrys punches himself in the nose until he bleeds.

The work of other performance artists is self-referential without having a body focus. New York artist Stuart Sherman objectifies his responses to acquaintances, cities, and so forth by creating short pieces of a minute or so. As himself he performs actions or gestures with props. The result is a language of ideas. In one of the approximately twenty short pieces comprising his *Seventh Spectacle* (1976), a cassette tape recorder says 'sh' several times as Sherman puts his finger to his lips in a silencing gesture and backs away from the sound. He puts on a necktie, and each time the recorder calls 'Stuart' Stuart Sherman, holding the end of the tie, pulls himself toward the machine. Reaching the machine the tape again calls 'Stuart' and he pushes the off button saying 'sh'. At one point in his *Tenth Spectacle: Portraits of Places* his impression of Toulouse/Lyon involves taking a telephone receiver from a flower pot and unscrewing the cap of the receiver, releasing rose petals.

Other performance artists draw more directly upon autobiographical material. Californian artist Linda Montano has designated portions of her actual everyday life as works of art. For example, in 1973 she sent announcements to her friends saying that she would stay home for a week and would be available. She photographed everyone who visited and documented food intake, telephone calls, and dreams. At the San Francisco Art Institute she

94.   The Kipper Kids

walked a treadmill for three hours, telling the story of her life into a micro-phone. In *Mitchell's Death* (1978) she shows a video tape of herself inserting acupuncture needles into her face as she performs live, with the needles in her face, by reading from an account she wrote about her responses to the death of her estranged husband by a self-inflicted gunshot wound. The account begins with the phone call telling her of his death and ends with her encounter with the corpse in a mortuary.

Some artists have realized their self-referential works as part of a theatre company. Director/playwright Lee Breuer of the Mabou Mines group in New York has written and staged a great variety of works including three productions he calls 'animations'. In the first of these, *The Red Horse Animation* (1971), three performers create an abstract image of a horse with their bodies. While speaking as a chorus they join their bodies in various ways until the horse takes shape, gallops, and then disintegrates. The perfor-

95. **Stuart Sherman** *Sixth Spectacle*, **photo: copyright © Babette Mangolte.**

mance, however, is an objectification of Breuer's creative process. The horse image and the apparent fragmented thoughts of the horse expressed through language are an objectification of Breuer's mental process as he attempts to create – his insecurities, his attempts to discover how he is related to objects and events in the world, and his attempts to discover his relationship to the work he is creating. This work and the animations which followed – *The B-Beaver Animation* and *The Shaggy Dog Animation* – are importantly self-reflexive.

Each of the three companies discussed in this section makes use of personal content in a distinctive way. The work of Richard Foreman evolves from a self-reflexive process similar to that of Lee Breuer's animations, but the results are quite different. Performer Spalding Gray and director Elizabeth LeCompte, working with other members of the Wooster Group (formerly the Performance Group), created the trilogy *Three Places in Rhode Island* in response to remembered events in Gray's life. And, as a solo performer, Spalding Gray presents autobiographical monologues drawing directly from his experiences. Squat Theatre in New York creates performances in the building where they live. The performers may play themselves, but the attitude of the audience is often ambivalent, not knowing if what seems to be actually is.

96. **Mabou Mines** *The Red Horse Animation*

In conventional realistic productions only the illusion has value, so the artists take care not to call attention to actualities in the real world. In some of the work discussed here part of the interest in the work derives from a juxtaposition of actual and illusionary elements.

Richard Foreman
The Ontological-Hysteric Theatre

Richard Foreman began his theatre in 1968 in order to stage his plays, which reflect his concern with consciousness and the structure of consciousness. His scripts are notations of his thoughts as he deals with the problems of making art. Because the scripts include his thoughts on his thinking, they contain warnings to himself, observations about why he has written a certain line or thought a particular idea. The process is thinking turned back on itself. But it is more than a writing process, it is a style of living which produces a style of thinking which leaves a residue of a certain style of writing.[1]

For Foreman writing is a continuous process. It does not begin and end for each play. When he is not actually rehearsing, he lies around the apartment with pen in hand reading, looking at pictures, making notes and diagrams in a notebook. The notes and diagrams become the text for a play. At a certain time he picks up one of his notebooks, looks through it and decides 'go from here to here and I have a play'. He does not change the order. Because the text for a play is extracted from the notebooks, it is a series of 'change-of-subjects' which Foreman believes has become the subject of the work itself. The continual change-of-subject, interruption, and re-beginning, reflects the true shape and texture of conscious experience which is the structure of the work.

Roughly, Foreman's work falls into two periods. Until about 1975 his interests tended to be phenomenological. He was interested, he says, in taking an object, 'putting it on stage, and finding different ways of looking at it – the object was there in isolation bracketted from the rest of the world'. In these early plays it was often the introduction of a new prop that 'refocused the energies'. There was no conventional cause-and-effect relationship of events. Images were repeated, sometimes with variations. Furniture and other objects were isolated by space so they seemed not to have a functional relationship, props were lowered and raised by cords defying the logic of our expectations, and loud buzzers separated one speech or phrase from another. The tempo was greatly attenuated as if each moment were being stretched. The spectator responding to these early works luxuriated in the prolongation of the moment.

In these early works Foreman used untrained performers whom he did not permit to be expressive in the traditional theatrical way. As director, Foreman attempted to control every detail of their movements. They walk, stand, sit, pick up furniture, but they do not express emotion. Similarly, the language, which is all on tape, is spoken without inflection – a different voice for each character – and heard over speakers as the performers go through the movements slowly almost as if they were sleepwalking. Occasionally a live performer echoes one or two words from the tape.

Total Recall (1970), one of these early phenomenological productions, has four principal character – Ben (identified with Foreman) and Hannah who are married, Hannah's relative Leo, and Sophia about whom Ben has visions. At the beginning of the play Ben is sitting at a table. The closet at the rear opens revealing Sophia standing inside holding a lamp. Hannah comes halfway through the door. Buzzer! Hannah says, 'I came in at the wrong moment.' Later Ben looks in the closet where the goddess Sophia hides. She reaches out and touches his face. Ben says, 'Art doesn't interest me like it used to. How come.' Much later, in the middle of the night, Hannah crosses the stage several times with Sophia under her nightgown. Foreman considers this one of many 'intrusions of the ludicrous' which are treated formally with slowness and composure.

About 1975 Foreman became less interested in presenting objects and figures in a phenomenological manner and more interested in 'capturing something of the blueprint quality' of his notebooks as they evolve, as he tries to notate each day where his obsessions are taking him. Increasingly he became interested in a form of theatre which, as a direct reflection of his notebooks, was a collection of fragments. The performances came to move faster because he was not interested in individual objects, but in 'the web of disruptions' as one thought displaces another. He became interested in whatever disrupted coherence. Beginning with *Pandering to the Masses: A Misrepresentation,* presented in his New York theatre in 1975, these disruptions were reflected in frequent and sudden changes to a new scene, a new locale. These scene changes are made by the performers in view of the spectators and are as much a part of the performance as other actions.

While the earlier slowed movement tended to put the spectator in a reduced state of consciousness somewhat like the work of Robert Wilson, Foreman's more recent focus on a rapid series of displacements or disruptions heightens spectator awareness. The stream of images passing at an accelerated rate makes one focus acutely so as not to miss anything. And because the images are so sensuous, one does not give up. In this conscious, active state one makes discoveries and connections, and sees formal relationships. These insights and intuitions occur in one's consciousness like sudden revelations producing a feeling of exhilaration.

The important thing, says Foreman, is not to succumb to the easy tendency to get carried away in some kind of emotional flow. In his daily life Foreman strives to be continuously self-aware, to be conscious of himself thinking and perceiving; and his performances are intended to stimulate the audience into a similar awareness. He sees this as a social and moral objective of his theatre – 'to force people to another level of consciousness' so that creative solutions are possible. This is accomplished by incorporating means which go against the audience's theatrically conditioned expectations, thus interrupting the flow. The voices on tape are detached from the figures on stage. The performers freeze in place and shift suddenly from fast to slow motion. They pull elastic cords to an object to give it focus and make the spectators conscious of where they are looking. A tape of Foreman's voice often comments on the performance. A buzzer or other sharp sound, so loud it is near the threshold of pain, is frequently sounded. Performers stare out of the stage picture at specific spectators, which makes them aware of themselves perceiving. Foreman believes that anything startling is an alienation device and serves to heighten consciousness.

Despite Foreman's interest in non-coherence, there is a vague situation in each play which none the less becomes a unifying element. In *Pandering to the Masses* the principal character Rhoda receives a letter with a red seal. It is an invitation to join a secret society which imparts a very special kind of knowledge. Although it is never clear what kind of knowledge is involved, the play focuses upon this invitation and her initiation into the society. Images of letters and envelopes appear in a variety of ways which also lend a compositional unity to the work.

Kate Manheim, who lives with Foreman and has been the principal performer in his productions since 1972, plays Rhoda, a character who appears in many of his plays. Rhoda lives with Max, another perennial character,

97. *Pandering to the Masses: A Misrepresentation*

who is a writer and seems to be analogous to Foreman; but, of course, all of the characters are fragments of the playwright since they speak only his thoughts and move according to his direction. The words are from his note-books where he has written thoughts triggered by his reading. The final speech in the play is spoken by Foreman's recorded voice: 'The meaning of the play', says the voice, 'will be found in the books scattered over the floor which include the text of *Pandering to the Masses: A Misrepresentation.*'

Although the productions consist of rapid-fire displacements reflecting Foreman's notations, they seem to have a coherence which probably is the structure of Foreman's thought processes. The entire procedure of making a production from notation to performance inevitably embodies the structure of the playwright–director's thinking. The sentences and gestures, Foreman says, 'write themselves' through him. Once he has chosen the notebook

98. *Pandering to the Masses*

99. *Pandering to the Masses*

100. *Pandering to the Masses*

section which will be the text and has distributed the words among several characters, he makes a tape recording with the chosen performers reading the lines without colouration. In rehearsals this tape becomes a kind of found-object-score to which he 'choreographs' the performers, scenery, objects, sounds, and music. When the production is nearly ready for performance, he may make a tape recording of himself expressing his thoughts in reaction to the work. These comments are played at the appropriate times during the course of the performance.

Foreman believes that the rehearsal procedure 'discovers the unity'; 'The natural course of things insists that things fall into some coherence'. Rather than unity being hard to achieve, the important task is 'to try to punch a few little holes in this continual insistence of the universe that there shall be coherence'.

In *le Livre des splendeurs,* presented in Paris in 1976, he again attempted to avoid a theme and simply displace one image with another in rapid succession. However, even this objective resulted in a unifying structure – a structure of displacements – and led to the development of a theme during rehearsals. The theme is implied in a speech added in rehearsal. At three points in the play Foreman's recorded voice says:

Ladies and Gentlemen, do you understand that an action is concluded and though one action does not lead to another, acts follow acts, discover-

164

ies follow discoveries, and one never stops inventing new ways to think about what one wants to think about.

The entire hour and forty-five minutes of *le Livre des splendeurs* consists of shifting images and associations punctuated by a buzzer, telephone bell, pings, and a loudly amplified sound resembling a cannon – all controlled by Foreman from his usual sound-control station in the first rows of the audience. Rhoda (Kate Manheim), who is naked most of the time, has various kinds of weights put on her body at different times in the play. A weight is put around her legs, a shoe with a large wooden block attached is put on her foot, a pole is strapped to her leg.

There is a home-made car resembling those of the 1920s. A naked woman lies at the front of the stage. As Max is about to leave in the car ('He resides in California with his mother.'), a pyramid of fruit is placed over the woman as a kind of *bon voyage* present. The Mother brings flowers in a large dish attached to her foot. Rhoda brings a large stack of books, staggering under the weight, but the car has gone.

A black weight one metre in diameter shaped like a potato is placed on top of Rhoda as she lies in bed. Max offers her a drink of water which he says will take away the pressure, but he drinks it instead and it gives him a pain which temporarily goes away when Rhoda asks for more weight. Eleanor is rolled on in a second bed, but when she tries to get out of it her foot is stuck. Water

101. *Le Livre des Splendeurs*

165

102. *Le Livre des Splendeurs*

is poured on the foot and Rhoda tumbles from her bed. Such surprising associations and connections continue throughout the play.

Rhoda is attacked by a 'wave of boredom'. She advises herself to 'accept it'.

> Don't let it know that you notice it even. Take it into your home and treat it comfortably. Subdue it with blankets and warm food.

At this point the voice of Foreman on tape announces that his name 'begins with a B. Boredom, is it not.'

Rhoda visits a Dentist who pulls strings from various parts of the stage to the painful tooth of his patient. But the Dentist himself sits in the chair, and Max becomes the dentist. He puts one end of a two-metre pole in Rhoda's

103. *Le Livre des Splendeurs*

104. *Le Livre des Splendeurs*

mouth and the other end in his own. Limbo music plays as they do a slow dance while raising and then lowering the pole with their mouths.

There are references to the complicated relationship of Foreman to Rhoda and the other characters in the play. The taped voice of Foreman, referring to Rhoda and Hannah, says:

> They are a disguise for somebody else who is writing about them: or – to be more exact: they are still two people, one of them the writer and one Rhoda; but Rhoda –

Rhoda is a special case in that she is always played by Manheim, who has had increasing impact upon the work. According to Foreman the plays have come to be built around her, 'around a not-me'.

Rhoda picks up Hannah on a street and asks for fifty dollars. As Rhoda bends over with her head in a purse, Hannah inspects her ass through a plastic bowl – or perhaps she is looking through Rhoda into the purse. Then Max is seen in a cafe paying two women who get into the car with him.

Mother, as a vendor of ice cream, gives Rhoda a red ice cream cone and she is ecstatic, rolling her eyes as in a trance and stumbling in jerks around the stage as five women with similar ice cream cones do a shuffling dance.

A doctor's table like a padded butcher's block is brought on stage and a naked woman straps the naked Rhoda to it.

A radio is brought on stage on a dog's leash. Max and Rhoda stab themselves but recover immediately. All of the other figures do a dance which ends with them stabbing themselves. Max opens a suitcase and books tumble out revealing knives underneath. 'It's diabolical', he says, 'how these things keep turning up when you least expect them' (Foreman-the-writer's observation on the image he has just noted about knives in a suitcase).

Finally, an empty cone is given to Rhoda who inspects it, then throws it down in utter disgust. She washes her hands and discovers something is written on the soap. Foreman's voice starts to tell her what is written when she interrupts him with another question which stops him. The final speech is by the Voice: 'One is always stopped, just as one starts finding out where it is that the messages are written.' The play ends with three pings.

The final speech, of course, is Foreman's reflection on the process of writing, not knowing where the sentences come from. It relates to an earlier speech spoken by Rhoda but expressing Foreman's thoughts as he tries to write. 'Order my pen to move,' she says, 'there's always an order coming from someplace.'

Foreman remains true to his thought process by following intuition during both the writing and staging. He does not compromise this process by rewriting or making choices dictated by theoretical or superego concerns. Nevertheless, some of the means employed have changed over the years. In *Penguin Touquet* (1981), presented at the New York Public Theatre, the performers were people of considerable acting experience – but, for the

105. *Le Livre des Splendeurs*

most part, that experience had been with alternative companies such as the Open Theatre and Mabou Mines. During the years she has worked with Foreman, Kate Manheim herself has developed a high level of skill and a distinct performance personality which has had an inevitable impact on the style of Ontological–Hysteric productions. However, her acting is unrelated to that demanded by conventional theatre. The performers in *Penguin Touquet* speak their lines live rather than on tape, sometimes talking simultaneously so it is not clear whose ideas are being expressed. But, of course, as always, they are Foreman's ideas.

In contrast to his writing since forming the Ontological–Hysteric Theatre, Foreman's work while studying playwriting at Yale University was quite different. His plays at that time came out of what he describes as an effort to write what the superego determined was right and professional and impressive. And a great deal of effort went into rewriting to eliminate what did not seem right. In other words he denied his own natural thoughts and structures. The turning point came when he discovered 'a new aesthetic built upon a truthfulness in attempting to catch the natural rhythms of the individual artist'. He learned to accept and make central to his work the very elements which he had previously tried to suppress. The writing process, he believes, 'skims the crest off the wave' of his living, and he then tries to retune his living to the process so that another crest of writing will emerge.

In performance Foreman makes the spectators conscious that they are perceiving, and the performance itself makes them aware of the playwright's thought processes as he wrote the script, as he staged it, and even his thoughts about the work after it was staged. He is in direct communication with the spectators. In a fundamental way the performance is about the mental process of making it.

Spalding Gray and Elizabeth LeCompte
The Wooster Group

Unique autobiographical productions have been created using memories and documentary material from the life of Spalding Gray. These have been 'composed' by Gray and director Elizabeth LeCompte. Gray plays himself in their trilogy with the collective title *Three Places in Rhode Island,* which consists of surreal images derived from group improvisations and incorporates more literal material such as recordings and slides of Gray's relatives. Although the productions derive from a personal focus, invented elements are integrated with the documentary in such a way that there is no clear distinction between the two.

Spalding Gray and Elizabeth LeCompte were members of Schechner's Performance Group when they began developing their own work. The Performance Group disbanded in 1980 and they, together with several other members of the company – Jim Clayburgh, Willem Dafoe, Libby Howes, and Ron Vawter – became known as the Wooster Group.

Before Spalding Gray joined the Performance Group in 1970 he had worked for five years as a traditional actor playing roles in plays written by others.[2] His Stanislavski training had taught him to imagine himself to be someone else. One of the means toward this end was to observe others. It was under Schechner's direction that Gray came to approach his work in a different way. Schechner stressed performance rather than acting. To him the performer was at least as important as the text. When he performed in the Performance Group production of *Mother Courage,* Gray says he developed the role without any conscious thought of what Brecht might have wanted, but instead 'made the role' out of his own 'immediate needs and let the text supply the structure for these personal actions'. It was the discovery of this way of working that led him to his autobiographical performances and the separation from Schechner.

Gray says that by nature he is 'extremely narcissistic and reflective'. He has always been self-conscious and aware of his everyday actions. He wanted to use these qualities toward creating his own work. As long as he played characters, even if developed through observations of people, he could 'only guess at knowing this other'. He realized he did not want to study others as objects, he wanted to explore himself as other. He no longer wanted to pretend to be a character outside himself. He wanted to perform his own actions and be reflective at the same time on stage before an audience. He says it became a kind of 'public confession of this reflectiveness. It became, "Look at me, I am one who sees himself seeing himself.'"

Elizabeth LeCompte, who had come to the Performance Group as assistant director to Schechner, began working with Gray and other performers in developing the autobiographical plays. She says that her interests in 'space and form and in the structure of a psychological performance' combine well with Gray's 'interest in performing, in confessing, showing himself'. For her the personal material has no special meaning, it is merely material to be used in making a structure. This detached view gave her the perspective necessary to direct the development of the trilogy and to structure it from performer improvisations and documentary material. She sees the work as being about Gray's 'love for the image of his mother [who committed suicide], and his attempt to re-possess her through his art'.

Each of the three plays comprising the trilogy is named after a place associated with Spalding Gray's past. *Sakonnet Point* (1975) is the name of the place where Gray spent his summers as a child. The piece was not planned in detail before rehearsals began, but he knew that he wanted to make a play about his growing up. He brought to each rehearsal objects with which to improvise. Most of the objects used in the performance are toys – an aeroplane, a few soldiers, a miniature garage, a toy house, a grove of tiny trees. The only objects used in all three of the plays making up the trilogy are a full-sized red camping tent, a record player, and the house.

The play was built entirely from free associations as the performers improvised with the objects. There is no attempt to tell a meaningful story. The movement is that of dreams or memory, and often is extended in time giving it a dream quality. Language is used rarely and is not in focus. There are the sounds of childhood. A woman's voice off-stage is heard calling 'Spalding' from time to time while Spalding Gray plays with toys. It is like the memory of being called by one's mother. An off-stage conversation of two women is heard, but we are unable to understand what is being said. There is the sound of a rocking chair rocking. A woman (Libby Howes) carries a small house. Later she hides it with her skirt and lies on top of it, protecting it with her body. *Sakonnet Point* ends with women hanging bed sheets on clotheslines. It is an image from Gray's childhood which makes connections with the childhood memories of the spectators.

The mother figure is even more important in *Rumstick Road* (1977), the second play of the trilogy, which takes its title from the address of the house where Gray grew up and his mother later committed suicide. The play concerns her suicide, and Gray believes it was his attempt to develop a meaningful structure into which he could place the meaningless act of suicide.

It was a confessional act. It was also an act of distancing. At last I was able to put my fears of, and identification with, my mother's madness into a theatrical structure. I was able to give it some therapeutic distance.

The materials with which the group began included letters written by

106. *Sakonnet Point*, **photo: Ken Kobland**

Gray's mother and father, old photographs of the family, and tape recordings he had made with his father, his two grandmothers, and the psychiatrist
who had treated his mother during her nervous breakdown. He had asked
them about his mother's suicide and how it had affected them. The
performers did group improvisations in reaction to this material.

The first scene of the play, after Gray has introduced himself to the
audience, consists of a farcical game of tag accompanied by lively music.
Gray chases The Woman (Libby Howes) whom we begin to think of as his
mother. They run in and out of a room slamming doors behind them. After
a time The Man (Ron Vawter), whom we associate with Gray's father,
appears with a gun and the two men struggle over it.

As the group worked with the tapes, using them as background for their
improvisations and exploring through improvisation some of the situations
described, surreal dream-like imagery emerged. In real life Gray's mother, a
Christian Scientist, believed that she had been visited by Christ and had
been healed by him. This led to an improvisation in which The Man attempts
to heal The Woman. The improvisation culminated in a scene in which
Gray, with a sheet over him, lies under a table. The Woman lies on the table.
The Man raises her dress exposing her mid-section and gives a lecture to the
audience about a process for relaxing the muscles of the torso. The lecture is
followed by a demonstration in which he massages The Woman's belly with
his hands and then with his lips, causing The Woman to laugh hysterically.

107. *Rumstick Road*

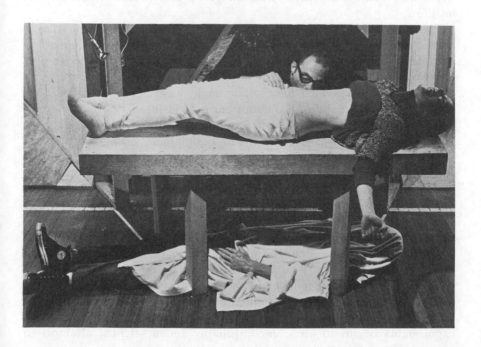

108. *Rumstick Road*

In performance the scene has no representational meaning so the audience can project on to it a number of associations. For example, it may suggest a child's interpretation of how his parents have sex, his imaginative assumptions about what goes on in his parents' bed when he hears his mother giggling. The scene also implies something about the relationship between Gray's parents. The Man presents his lecture as if The Woman were only an illustrative object.

The play also makes use of letters from members of Gray's family and photographs of them. At one point a slide of the house on Rumstick Road is projected on the wall and The Woman violently throws her head back and forth in a kind of mad dance. Finally, exhausted, she seems to hold onto the roof of the house for support. In another scene a slide of Gray's mother is projected onto the face of The Woman while she recites a letter written by Gray's mother.

A tape-recorded conversation about his mother's suicide between Gray and his father is played as The Man and Gray, seated in chairs, pantomime and lip-sync to the tape. Then Gray makes a telephone call and talks live to the previously recorded voice of the psychiatrist who treated his mother. The play ends with Gray reading a letter from his father.

The performance has a quality of personal revelation even though there are images which cannot be literally autobiographical. The line between documentary and imagination is intentionally blurred. The play is a collective work resulting, as Gray says, from 'group associations around facts in my life'.

The inceptive idea for *Nayatt School* (1978), the third play in the trilogy, grew out of Gray's interest in social themes relating to madness, anarchy, and the loss of innocence. He was also very interested in T.S. Eliot's play *The Cocktail Party* and particularly the character of Celia Coplestone whom Gray fantasized was what his mother might have been if she had been capable of intellectual distance about her nervous breakdown. The group began workshops with young boys. Eventually two boys and two girls were involved in the performances with the four adult members of the group.

The setting for *Nayatt School* appears to be a rear view of the room in *Rumstick Road*. The audience seating is raised about three metres so they look down into the space. At the beginning of the performance, Gray sits at a table on the audience level speaking directly to them about *The Cocktail Party,* and he plays portions from a recording of the play. Then the focus shifts to the room below which has a transparent roof and a window through which the action can be seen. It is used as a surreal doctor's office in which three scenes take place. First a dentist (Spalding Gray) drills holes in a patient who is the former lover of the dentist's wife. Then The Woman (Libby Howes) is given an examination for breast cancer after being wrapped in butcher paper. Finally, a chicken heart which has been used for experiments begins to grow uncontrollably and a scientist attempts to prevent it from destroying the world.

109. *Rumstick Road*

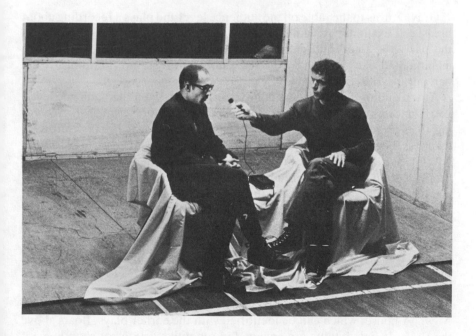

110. *Rumstick Road*

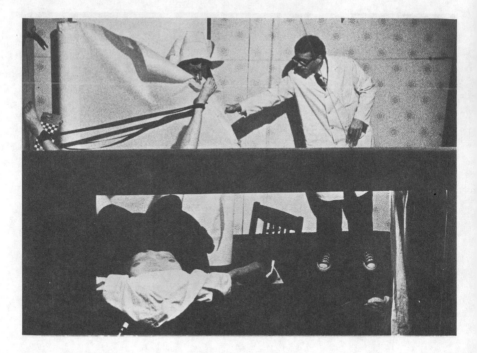

111.   *Nayatt School*

Gray returns to the table on the audience level and plays a recording about breast self-examination while the lower level is set up for a cocktail party. At the party the four children are dressed and made-up as adults; they are manipulated like puppets by the real adults in the group. Periodically the party erupts into chaos.

At the end of the play, the adult performers, now on the audience level, partly undress and destroy the records in a fit of chaotic eroticism. According to Gray, the play does not talk about madness, it breaks into total madness, becoming the inside of a person's head.

While *Three Places in Rhode Island* was created collectively and therefore properly should be considered group work, its focus is Spalding Gray's life and his sensibilities. It expresses through abstract images and various forms of documentation how Gray feels about events in his life and how other members of the company feel about similar events in their lives. It is about the experience of growing up and living as a middle-class American. The three plays, says Gray, 'are not just about the loss of my mother but about the feeling of loss itself. I have had this feeling for as long as I can remember.'

The company made an 'epilogue' to the trilogy called *Point Judith* (1979) in which the main portion is a response to O'Neill's *Long Day's Journey into Night*. A house, which can be identified with the earlier plays, floats above the floor. Its inhabitants are engaged in repetitive actions of chaotic madness. There is no dialogue in this section, but many surreal visual images,

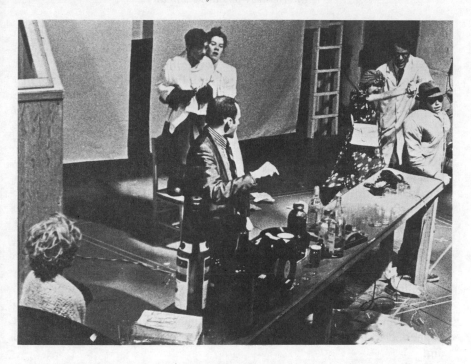

112.   *Nayatt School*

including film projections, which create a metaphor for the destruction of the American family.

By the time of *Point Judith* the company productions were no longer explicitly personal. The more literal autobiographical material from Spalding Gray's life was being used in monologues composed by Gray and presented by him alone sitting behind a table and speaking directly to the audience in the first person. He considers these as extensions of his direct speech in *Rumstick Road* when he introduced himself to the audience and later described the house in which he and his family had lived. Each of the monologues runs about an hour and fifteen minutes and centres on a particular theme or period in his life. They are not written and not memorized, but for each monologue Gray has decided which events will comprise the performance.

The monologues were composed in an order approximating the chronology of the events in his life. *Sex & Death to the Age of 14* (1979) deals with his discoveries as he passed through puberty – the deaths of pets and their burial in an animal cemetery, discovery of sex in the form of his father's pornography and adolescent names for sexual organs. *Booze, Cars, & College Girls* (1979) concerns the period from post-puberty to young adulthood. He describes his experiences with alcohol, his temporary interest in becoming a race driver, his loss of virginity, and his loss of a lover. In *India & After*

(America), presented in the same year, Gray recalls his experiences while on tour with the Performance Group and his return to the United States. It was during this period that he thought he was going mad, but like the other monologues this one is mainly comic in tone. For a time he was an actor in a pornographic film in order to make money to travel west. In las Vegas he was arrested because he refused to give a policeman his name. *A Personal History of the American Theatre* (1980) is presented with the aid of forty-seven cards on which are printed the names of the plays in which Gray acted between 1960 and 1970. The cards are in a random order. Drawing one at a time he reminisces about events surrounding the plays, the actors in them, theatre anecdotes, and personal problems. After the monologue, the audience was invited to talk to him about the photos and other theatre memorabilia he had brought with him. *Points of Interest (America)*, first presented in San Francisco in 1980, draws upon his experiences driving across the United States from New York to perform at the San Francisco International Theatre Festival. He describes love-making episodes with his travelling companion, people along the way, visits to a sensory deprivation tank, a U.F.O. meeting when the speaker failed to show up, and his living circumstances while performing in San Francisco. Finally, he relates what happened to him today, and concludes with, 'That was today. And here I am.'

Ending with the present moment is just one of the means Gray uses to bring focus to the present so that the performance is not merely a relating of past events. It is important that the spectator does not have the sense that Gray is 'acting', but rather that he is speaking to them about real events. His style of delivery is flat, uncoloured, and candid. He really looks at spectators, especially when they react to something he has said. He actually reflects while in front of them rather than speaking memorized lines and pretending to reflect. He has incorporated various devices into his performances to make reflection necessary. The random order of the play titles in *A Personal History of the American Theatre* helps assure that he reflects on the events rather than falling into a repetition of previous performances. In *India & After (America)* he introduced a more complicated practice. An assistant, sitting at a table beside him, opens a dictionary to a random page, selects a word and its definition and calls out a time from fifteen seconds to four minutes. Gray then speaks for that length of time on an episode suggested by the word. For example, 'somnolent' reminded him of his inability to get an erection while making a pornographic film. This process continues throughout the entire performance.

All of his work, Gray says, has been made to satisfy his personal needs. *Sakonnet Point* came from a need to think about his childhood. An obsession about his mother's suicide led to *Rumstick Road*. His need to have children resulted in *Nayatt School* which provided the opportunity to work closely with boys and girls. His monologues, of course, were a direct means of thinking through various troubling events in his past. However, despite the dwelling on personal problems, the tone of the monologues is predominantly comic because of a distanced, ironic perspective. The audience may sense how Gray felt while undergoing the experiences, but now he is alive in front of them having survived to tell about them from an objective perspective. Furthermore, the archetypical American experiences – love, sex, booze, cars, embarrassing situations – are recognized by the audience as similar to their own. A kind of catharsis takes place, and an important connection is made between the performer and the spectators.

Ideally, says Gray, a performance would deal with the present in the room where the performance is taking place. He would simply enter and start talking about the events taking place in the room. Although he has not actually presented such a performance, his monologues are the most literally autobiographical work that has been presented in the theatre. Although talking about past events, he is present as himself before the audience, living the most recent segment of his life.

Squat Theatre

The expatriate Hungarian company known as Squat Theatre have erased the distinction between life and art. They live and perform in the same space – a building with a storefront window looking onto a busy New York street. Those who pass outside become part of the performance for those inside and vice versa. Although members of the company sometimes wear bizarre costumes, they perform actions as themselves rather than as characters. And they take risks which have potential consequences for their lives.[3]

Originally the group formed in 1969 at the Kassák Culture House in Budapest. In 1972 the group's licence to perform was withdrawn on the grounds that it was 'obscene' and 'apt to be misinterpreted from a political point of view'. Being unable to give further performances in public, they began performing in the fifth floor apartment of members Péter Halász and Anna Koós and became the Kassák Apartment Theatre. During the next four years they also performed in a disused country chapel, a sand pit, and on an island.

In the autumn of 1973 the group performed at the Open Theatre Festival in Wroclaw, Poland, without an invitation. The play used some elements from earlier work including nudity, the cutting of a vein in the wrist, and the drinking of blood mixed with milk. When they returned to Budapest the passports of three members were withdrawn. In 1976 the group succeeded in leaving Hungary, and after performing for a year in Western Europe, the group of eleven adults and five children settled permanently in New York.

The first performances in the United States were of *Pig, Child, Fire!* (1977). It takes its name from three elements the group intended to use in the performance. They were unable to get a pig, however, so they substituted a small goat. The events take place in real-world time, rather than condensed dramatic time, and therefore seem to happen very slowly. While the four parts of the play are presented in the same order, there is no attempt to duplicate exactly a previous performance.

In the first part, 'Stavrogin's Confessions – Dostoevsky's *The Devils*', recorded music is playing as the curtain rises revealing a twice-life-size figure of a man hanging upside down with a normal-size head protruding from its anus. The small head, identical to the large one, is suspended by a rope around its neck. Tethered at one side of the stage is a live goat with a child's mask on its forehead. A little girl plays while the goat chews on various objects. A woman in red (Anna Koós) smokes a cigar. She chops up a head of cabbage with an axe, the little girl plays with a knife. The entire rear wall of the performance space is glass and other spectators can be seen looking in. A man (Péter Halász) with a long black beard appears outside. One arm of his overcoat is in flames. After watching for a time he moves on. (The overcoat, like most objects used in the play, has a history. It was worn by the actor's grandfather in the First World War.)

The woman begins to read Stavrogin's confessions from Dostoevsky's *The Devils*. (Stavrogin feels guilty because of a child's suicide by hanging.) The reading is taken over by the woman's taped voice, then by the voice of a man. As the little girl plays with the goat, the woman unwraps a package of assorted animal viscera. Some of the innards she arranges on the table, paints them red, and flours them. She then holds the goat on her lap, lays large pieces of meat on its back, slices them, and sprinkles them with flour. The man with the black beard, accompanied by a police dog, peers through the glass and moves on.

The woman stands the little girl on a chair, and puts make-up and a wig on her. From inside her own dress she takes a pair of plastic woman's breasts and ties them around the child's chest. The man with the dog appears again. The taped reading of the confessions stops. The first words of dialogue are spoken – the man protests that the document was incomplete and inaccurate. The woman pounds on the glass and the man opens his overcoat. He is naked. He leaves quickly.

The woman pulls away the giant figure leaving a man (Pétr Brežnyik) hanging by his neck, an erect penis protruding from his flies. As the body convulses, the man ejaculates. He removes his mask to reveal an identical real face beneath, then he dies. As German dance music plays, the woman clasps the man's swinging body. Then she cuts the goat's rope and carries the animal off with the child following. The man with the dog is now inside. He looks around.

In part two, 'Dinner and Nous Sommes les Mannequins', two television monitors face the audience and a third is outside where a woman and four children are eating dinner and talking. The inside area is dark, but one can make out a man slumped over a table. A woman in red sits by the glass looking out. A video camera pans the inside and outside spectators and their images are seen on the monitors. A car drives into the dinner table as the diners scatter. A man in a trenchcoat and hat gets out of the back seat. An

113. *Pig, Child, Fire!*

identically dressed man enters. The two draw guns, aim at each other, and stand frozen. The woman in red draws a gun and shoots the man closest to her, and the second man shoots her. The gunman comes inside to the man slumped over the table, sharpens an axe on an electric grinder, and chops off the man's hand. The slumped man sits up startled and pulls a bloody stump from his sleeve revealing his undamaged hand. He pulls a gun and tries to shoot the gunman, but it is only a toy. Submissively, he stands on the table, drops his pants, kneels down and sticks the gun in his anus. He fires the toy gun and falls forward, ass in the air. The gunman puts his trenchcoat over the bare posterior with the protruding gun.

The third part is 'Letter to André Breton by Antonin Artaud, February 1947'. Anna Koós stands outside behind a lectern. A video camera and a small spotlight are under her skirt on the ground between her feet focused on the naked crotch. The image is transmitted to the television monitors. During the eight minutes it takes to read the Artaud letter, small but visible changes can be seen in the projected image.

The fourth part, 'The Last One', was originally presented in the group's Budapest apartment in May 1972. A man stands eating a piece of bread. A second man enters with a pane of glass which he measures and cuts. Neither speaks.

The play contains no set dialogue. Except for the readings of Dostoevsky and Artaud very little is spoken. The group's ideas are developed through discussion and as they consider the possibilities of the space in which they are

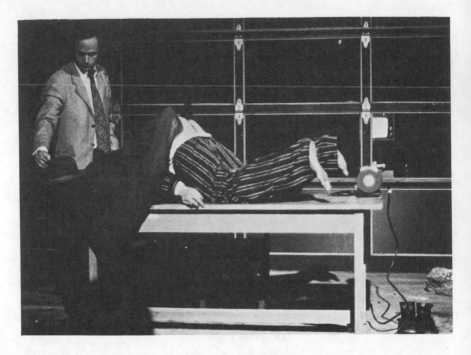

114. *Pig, Child, Fire!*

to perform. For example, when they went to Rotterdam to make the first performance of *Pig, Child, Fire!* they found an empty store with living space upstairs. They conceived of the idea of using the glass storefront to allow the audience inside to see spectators who gathered on the sidewalk outside and vice versa.

The glass division also relates to some of the group's theoretical ideas. In their view, since the ancient performances of Greek tragedy there has not been a unity between the cosmic drama presented by the performers and the private-life drama of the spectators. They believe that actors have become mere vehicles for ideas and ideologies which remain separated from the lives of both performers and spectators. In an age when there is no engulfing cosmic drama (mythology) inextricably relating people and events, Squat is committed to presenting the resultant abyss. They accept this abyss as the present day universal cosmic drama; they live in it and they present it.

When the group decided to settle permanently in New York, they needed a space that would be both their home and their performance space. And it had to have a shop window facing the street. They found a suitable building on West 23rd Street. *Andy Warhol's Last Love* (1978) was their first work to be made in the United States. In a sense it is two plays – one that is seen by the paying spectators inside the theatre and one seen free by those passing on the sidewalk outside. Seeing each other through the glass window, the two audiences become part of the performance for each other. The inter-

115. *Pig, Child, Fire!*

mingling of actual elements with fictional illusion, of living and art, is a
dominant characteristic of *Andy Warhol's Last Love* as it was of *Pig, Child,
Fire!*

Squat Theatre has been compared to Pirandello because of its different
levels of illusion. But there is an important difference. In Pirandello's plays,
although one illusion may be replaced by another, we are not permitted to
focus on the actual performer in the present; we perceive only the fictional
characters in a fictional time and place. Squat Theatre intermingles actuality
and illusion in such a way that actual persons and events become more
mysterious and fictional ones seem more real.

The first section of *Andy Warhol's Last Love*, 'Aliens on the Second
Floor', immediately blurs the line between actuality and theatrical inven-
tion. The spectators enter the room where group members Eva Buchmüller
and Istvan Balint live. Their personal belongings are there. Buchmüller and
Balint are also there engaged in natural activities. He is lying on the bed, she
is sitting at the table listening to a radio and nervously twisting her hair as she
does both on and off stage. From time to time she changes the station and the
audience hears whatever is actually being broadcast at the time. Gradually
fictional elements are introduced. The voice of Ulrike Meinhof is heard over
the radio speaking for the Intergalaxy 21 Revolutionary Committee. (A
disco formerly in the building was called Galaxy 21.) She instructs the listen-
ers to make their deaths public so they can be provided with new bodies and

183

116. *Andy Warhol's Last Love*

taken away to the planet where she now lives. Other bizarre events take place. The hem of the dressing gown Buchmüller is wearing is nailed to the floor and she is shot. A table cloth burns and a man rolls out from under the table in flames. And at the end of the scene a woman from space (Anna Koós) enters to resurrect the dead Buchmüller. She wears a silver cloak and has an erect penis protruding from the dress covering her belly which is very large with an actual pregnancy.

The rest of the play takes place in the main room on the ground floor which is separated from the street by the glass storefront. Members of Squat have said that they came to realize while still in their Budapest apartment that when they looked into the windows of other apartments, natural everyday actions took on a theatrical quality. Like a mirror or the frame of a picture, viewing objects and events through a transparent separation helps to set them apart from the everyday world so they become objects and events for perception and seem to lose their efficacy. The window also directs our focus, making it difficult for us to ignore what is happening on the other side. Although on the street we would feel awkward looking at a stranger for more than a fleeting moment, we stare unflinchingly at the person through the window. We perceive others and we perceive others perceiving us without embarrassment. But it is not simply the window that makes staring acceptable; in the theatre – etymologically 'a place for seeing'

– it is as acceptable to look at spectators who are made objects of perception by the window as it is to look at the other performers.

The window, which allows New York to present itself, is a metaphor for our relationship to our peopled world, our distanced voyeur-like relationship which permits us to observe without being touched, to experience vicariously the events around us. Andy Warhol exemplifies this relationship and other American attitudes and values. He is rich and famous, he is a television addict, he is seemingly uninvolved and uncommitted. He says in *The Philosophy of Andy Warhol* that when he got his first TV set he stopped caring about having close relationships. Until he was shot, he always thought he was watching TV rather than living life. When he got his tape recorder it ended whatever emotional life he still had 'because a problem just meant a good tape, and when a problem transforms itself into a good tape it's not a problem any more'. He experiences events vicariously through television, by interviewing others, and by encouraging friends to phone him and tell him what is happening. By avoiding and distancing what might affect him, he remains unaffected.

Warhol is the principal figure in the film which comprises the second part of *Andy Warhol's Last Love*. It begins with the video portion of an actual TV commercial message by Crazy Eddie who is giving a pitch for the television sets, tape recorders, and other electronic equipment which surround him in one of his stores. The audio portion is a hyped-up reading of Kafka's brief narrative 'An Imperial Message', which tells the story of a messenger unsuccessfully attempting to bring 'you' the whispered message of the dying emperor. Although the messenger may go on for thousands of years, through the crowd at the emperor's deathbed, down the stairs, through the courtyards, even to the outer gates of the palace, he still would have the capital city with its refuse before him and no one can force a way through that. 'But you sit at your window when evening falls and dream it to yourself.' A performer wearing a life-like mask of Andy Warhol rides a horse through the deserted streets of Manhattan's financial district. Events occur – a girl raises her skirt for him, a man is shot, a man with his face half burned passes on the street – but the artist on his horse gallops along unseeing, untouched, and unmoved. On the film we see him arrive in front of Squat Theatre, and then live he enters the theatre.

For Squat Theatre Andy Warhol is a tragic hero who in his films searched for an ideal of making living event and artistic form inseparable; but like the alternative culture of the sixties with its similar aims, he succumbed to the powerful anti-spiritual counter-revolutionary forces of the present. The last ten or fifteen years have proved, according to Squat, that the ideal was unattainable. In the hands of Warhol art became banal and reproducible, failing to express the essence of life. It is not useful for the artist to focus on the unachievable ideals: such a utopian focus keeps the artist uninvolved, an observer at an emotional distance. The focus of the artist must be on what is, not on what should be. The counter-revolutionary forces cannot be negated by artistic idealism. But if the only value of an artist's work is his own material gain, if this is the function of art, then Crazy Eddie is one of the greatest. Furthermore, his message is as useful as that of the utopian artist or the secret deathbed message of Kafka's emperor. Squat does not believe that theatre can transmit a message, especially not one from elsewhere – not even from writer to audience. Like the message of the emperor, it is never received.

When the performer masked as Warhol enters the theatre from West 23rd Street he is accompanied by performer Kathleen Kendel. The final section of the play, 'Interview with the Dead', begins. She removes her cloak and, naked, performs an incantation calling up various spirits. The curtain over the window, on which the film was projected, is pulled aside and throughout the rest of the performance the actual people and events of West 23rd Street become part of the play. And spectators who gather outside can see in.

In the interview which follows actuality and illusion are again indistinct. As Warhol and Kendel sit at the table passing a microphone back and forth, a taped voice claiming to be Warhol asks questions of the real Kendel who answers live and extemporaneously insisting that she is an actual witch. Among the actual spectators visible outside through the storefront window is the man seen burning upstairs in the first scene and again in the film. His face is burned, but some spectators do not realize that he is a performer. As the interview progresses a video camera outside transmits to a television screen inside scenes from the street – the faces of individual spectators, cars passing, the Empire State Building (actually a model) burning. The TV screen gives everything – actual and fictional – the same distanced sense of reality. From among the spectators outside Ulrike Meinhof enters. She carries out the sentence of the Intergalaxy 21 Revolutionary Committee. Warhol is 'shot for his merits'. (It was almost exactly ten years before that the real Andy Warhol was shot.) The woman from space with her silver cloak, pregnant belly, and erect penis enters from the street to take Warhol to her planet.

At the end of the performance a mylar mirror is lowered from the ceiling in front of the inside audience. We become conscious of looking at ourselves as we have been looking at those outside. But, like Warhol, we have been observing the people and events of New York from the secure, removed position of voyeurs. However, there is another irony. While inside we may think of ourselves as voyeurs exploiting the drunks, kids, and Chelsea Hotel clients who pass by and become our entertainment, outside the spectators are talking, smoking, some drinking or eating, moving around freely, generally having a good time watching the antics of a naked woman and a man who looks like Warhol. They see rows of spectators sitting stiffly on chairs. They look rather silly, and they paid five dollars to get in. Both audiences have a vicarious experience and there seems to be no risk.

For the Squat company, however, there is considerable risk. They are a small community outside the larger society in which they live, but they are

117. *Andy Warhol's Last Love*

118. *Andy Warhol's Last Love*

not free from its impact. They take physical and legal risks and, like Ulrike Meinhof, they are anarchists – not political but aesthetic. They are audacious in their confrontation with oppressive aesthetic views which

119. *Andy Warhol's Last Love*

120. *Andy Warhol's Last Love*

separate art and life. For them art and life are intertwined, and consequently they risk more and more artists. They take physical risks with fire and have been threatened by those passing in the street – by both spectators and police. They risk being arrested for any number of charges from breaking fire regulations to obstructing the sidewalk, to indecent exposure and the corruption of minors. And there is the risk of being deported as undesirable aliens.

Instead of conveying a message about life that is not theirs, Squat believes theatre is a living, ongoing event in which no distinction is made between performer and character. They are not carrying a message from elsewhere. The performers do not play characters from a source outside themselves; they are themselves even if they wear bizarre costumes. To Squat this is the essence of theatre, that art and living overlap.

References

2 Primary Explorations

1. Kenneth H. Brown, *The Brig*, With an Essay on The Living Theatre by Julian Beck and Director's Notes by Judith Malina (New York: Hill and Wang, 1965) p. 24.

2. *Ibid.*, p. 83.

3. *Ibid.*, p. 24.

4. Julian Beck, 'How to Close a Theatre', *Tulane Drama Review* (T23), VIII, 3 (Spring 1964) 181.

5. Pierre Biner, *The Living Theatre*, translated from the French by Robert Meister (New York: Avon Books, 1972) pp. 234-48.

6. Julian Beck, '3 Stages in the Genesis of *Frankenstein*, A Dramatic Spectacle Created by the Living Theatre Company', *City Lights Journal*, 3 (1966) 70.

7. Biner, *The Living Theatre*, p. 159.

8. Lyon Phelps, 'Brecht's *Antigone* at the Living Theatre', *The Drama Review* (T37), XII, 1 (Fall 1967) 128.

9. All quotations from *Paradise Now* are from Judith Malina and Julian Beck, *Paradise Now;* Collective Creation of the Living Theatre (New York: Vintage Books, 1971).

10. Aldo Rostagno with Julian Beck and Judith Malina, *We, The Living Theatre*, A Pictorial Documentation by Gianfranco Mantegna . . . of *Mysteries and Smaller Pieces, Antigone, Frankenstein, Paradise Now* (New York: Ballantine Books, Inc., 1970) pp 37, 25.

11. Biner, *The Living Theatre*, pp. 225–7.

12. All information about the work of the Living Theatre in Brazil is from my discussions with them in November 1971 unless otherwise noted. See Theodore Shank, 'The Living Theatre in Brazil', *Praxis, A Journal of Radical Perspectives on the Arts*, I, 1 (Spring 1975) 66–72.

13. Julian Beck and Judith Malina, 'From *The Legacy of Cain:* Favela Project No.

1 – *Christmas Cake for the Hot Hole and the Cold Hole*, A Collective Creation of The Living Theatre', *Scripts*, I 1 (November 1971) 5–16.

14. Letter to Theodore Shank from Judith Malina, Pittsburgh, 3 January 1975.

15. Julian Beck, Charles Derevere, Judith Malina and William Shari, interviewed by Erika Munk, 'The Living Theatre and the Wobblies', *Performance*, I, 6 (May/June 1973) 90.

16. Ross Wetzsteon, 'The Living Theatre at the Pittsburgh Station', *Village Voice* (New York), 21 April 1975.

17. Information about their work in Italy is from an interview with Judith Malina and Julian Beck in London, 23 July 1979.

18. Renfrau Neff, *The Living Theatre: USA* (Indianapolis and New York: The Bobbs–Merrill Company, 1970) p. 74.

19. *Ibid.*, pp. 233–4.

20. *Ibid.*, pp. 234–5.

21. Robert Pasoli, *A Book on the Open Theatre* (New York: Bobbs–Merrill Company, Inc., 1970) p. 83.

22. Unless otherwise indicated, information is from my interviews with Joseph Chaikin, Raymond Barry, Shami Chaikin, Ellen Maddow, Jo Ann Schmidman, Tina Shepard, and Paul Zimet in London in June 1973, and from London performances of *Terminal, Mutation Show*, and *Nightwalk*, June 1973.

23. Susan Yankowitz, *Terminal, in Scripts*, I, 1 (November 1971) 17–45; and Roberta Sklar, *'Terminal:* an Interview', by Paul Ryder Ryan, *The Drama Review* (T51), XV 3 (Summer 1971) 149–57.

3 Theatre of Social Change

1. 'Interview: Charles Ludlam', *Performing Arts Journal*, III, 1 (Spring–Summer 1978) 78–9.

2. Joan Holden, 'Comedy and Revolution', *Arts in Society,* VI 3 (Winter 1969).

3. Unless otherwise noted, all information from Joan Holden is from my conversations with her (1970–80).

4. 'El Teatro Campesino; Interviews with Luis Valdez,' by Beth Bagby, *The Drama Review* (T36), XI, 4 (Summer 1967) 74–5.

5. Unless otherwise noted, all quotations are from my conversations with Luis Valdez (1965–80).

6. Luis Valdez, *Actos* (San Juan Bautista, California: El Centro Campesino Cultural, 1971) pp. 1–2.

7. An Interview with Luis Valdez by Charles Pelton, 'Zoot-Suiting to Hollywood; Teatro Campesino's Luis Valdez', *Artbeat* (San Francisco, December 1980) p. 28.

4 Environmental Theatre

1. Some of the information in this section is from my correspondence and conversations with Richard Schechner beginning about 1967.

2. '6 Axioms for Environmental Theatre', *The Drama Review* (T39), XII 3 (Spring 1968) 41–64.

3. 'An Interview with Grotowski' by Richard Schechner, *The Drama Review* (T41), XIII, 1 (Fall 1968) 34.

4. Richard Schechner (ed.), *Dionysus in 69; The Performance Group* (New York: Farrar, Straus and Giroux, 1970).

5. 'External Order, Internal Intimacy; an Interview with Jerzy Grotowski', by Marc Fumaroli, *The Drama Review* (T45), XIV, 1 (Fall 1969) 173; and Margaret Croyden, 'Notes from the Temple: A Grotowski Seminar', *The Drama Review* (T45), XIV, 1 (Fall 1969) 181.

6. Richard Schechner, *Essays on Performance Theory, 1970–1976* (New York: Drama Book Specialists, 1977) pp. 29–30. Also a letter to Theodore Shank from Richard Schechner, New York, 17 April 1971. See also Schechner's adaptation, *Makbeth; After Shakespeare* (Schulenburg, Texas: I.E. Clark, 1978).

7. Letter to Theodore Shank from Richard Schechner, New York, 17 April 1971.

8. John Lahr, 'On-Stage', *The Village Voice* (New York), 31 December 1970, p. 50.

9. Francoise Kourilsky, 'Dada and Circus', *The Drama Review* (T61, March 1974) pp. 104–9.

10. Unless otherwise noted, information attributed to Peter Schumann is from letters or conversations with him beginning in 1969.

11. Peter Schumann, 'With the Bread & Puppet Theatre: An Interview', by Helen Brown and Jane Seitz, *The Drama Review* (T38), XII, 2 (Winter 1968) 63, 66.

12. Peter Schumann, quoted in Florence Falk, 'Bread and Puppet: *Domestic Resurrection Circus*', *Performing Arts Journal*, II, 1 (Spring 1977) 22.

13. Information about Snake Theater is from my conversations with Laura Farabough and Christopher Hardman beginning in 1974, and from Hardman's presentation for the Experimental Panel I organized for the American Theatre Critics Association, 24 May 1980, in San Francisco.

5 New Formalism

1. Allan Kaprow, *Assemblage, Environments & Happenings* (New York: Harry N. Abrams, Inc., 1966) p. 201.

2. This concept is discussed in Bill Simmer's 'Robert Wilson and Therapy', *The Drama Review* (T69), XX, 1 (March 1976) 99–110.

3. The text of *I Was Sitting on My Patio/This Guy Appeared I Thought/I Was Hallucinating* has been published in *Performing Arts Journal* (10/11), IV, 1 and 2 (1979) 200–18.

4. Robert Wilson, 'I Thought I Was Hallucinating', *The Drama Review* (T76), XXI, 4 (December 1977) 76.

5. Michael Kirby, 'Manifesto of Structuralism', *The Drama Review* (T68), XIX, 4 (December 1975) 82–3, and 'Structural Analysis/Structural Theory', *The Drama Review* (T72), XX, 4 (December 1976) 51–68.

6. Michael Kirby, 'Structuralism Redefined', *Soho Weekly News* (New York), 22 July 1976, p. 13.

6 Self as Content

1. Information about Richard Foreman is from my conversations and recorded interviews with him, and letters from him, beginning in 1970; and from his 'How I Write My (Self: Plays)', *The Drama Review* (T76), XXI, 4 December 1977) pp. 5–24.

2. Information and quotations concerning Spalding Gray and Elizabeth LeCompte are from my conversations and recorded interviews with them and from the following: Spalding Gray, 'About *Three Places in Rhode Island*', in *The Drama Review* (T81), XXIII, 1 (March 1979) 31–42; Elizabeth LeCompte and Spalding Gray, 'The Making of a Trilogy', *Performing Arts Journal*, III, 2 (Fall 1978) 81–91;

References

and Elizabeth LeCompte interview on 'Acting/Non-Acting' by Scott Burton, *Performance Art Magazine* 2 (New York) 14–16.

   3. Historical information about Squat Theatre is from the company.

Bibliography

1. The Alternative Theatre
The best sources are the following periodicals:
The Drama Review (1955–67 called *Tulane Drama Review)*
  721 Broadway, Room 600, New York, N.Y. 10003, U.S.A.
Performing Arts Journal
  P.O. Box 858, Peter Stuyvesant Station, New York, N.Y. 10009, U.S.A.
Theater (formerly *Yale/Theater)*
  Box 2046 Yale Station, New Haven, Connecticut 06520, U.S.A.
Banes, Sally, *Terpsichore in Sneakers: Post-Modern Dance* (Boston: Houghton Mifflin Co., 1980) 292 pages.
Goldberg, RoseLee, *Performance: Live Art 1909 to the Present* (New York: Harry N. Abrams, Inc., 1979) 128 pages.
Kaprow, Allan, *Assemblage, Environments, and Happenings* (New York: Harry Abrams, 1966) 342 pages.
Kirby, Michael, *Happenings; an Illustrated Anthology* (New York: E.P. Dutton, 1965) 288 pages.
——, *The Art of Time; Essays on the Avant-Garde* (New York: E.P. Dutton, 1969) 255 pages.
Kostelanetz, Richard, *The Theatre of Mixed Means; An Introduction to Happenings, Kinetic Environments, and Other Mixed-Means Performances* (New York: The Dial Press, 1968) 311 pages.
—— (ed.), *Esthetics Contemporary* (New York: Prometheus Books, 1978) 444 pages.
Loeffler, Carl E. (ed.), *Performance Anthology: Source Book for a Decade of California Performance Art* (San Francisco: Contemporary Arts Press, 1980) 500 pages.
Marranca, Bonnie (ed.), *The Theatre of Images* (New York: Drama Books Specialists, 1977) 256 pages.

2. Primary Explorations

THE LIVING THEATRE

Beck, Julian, *The Life of the Theatre* (San Francisco: City Lights Books, 1972).

Biner, Pierre, *The Living Theatre*, translated from the French by Robert Meister (New York: Avon Books, 1972) 256 pages.

Brown, Kenneth H., *The Brig*, With an Essay on The Living Theatre by Julian Beck and Director's Notes by Judith Malina (New York: Hill and Wang, 1965) 107 pages.

Malina, Judith, *The Enormous Despair*. Her diary August 1968–April 1969 (New York: Random House, 1972) 249 pages.

—— and Julian Beck, *Paradise Now:* Collective Creation of The Living Theatre (New York: Vintage Books, 1971) 154 pages.

Rostagno, Aldo, with Julian Beck and Judith Malina, *We, The Living Theatre*, A Pictorial Documentation by Gianfranco Mantegna . . . of *Mysteries and Smaller Pieces, Antigone, Frankenstein, Paradise Now* (New York: Ballantine Books, Inc., 1970) 240 pages.

THE OPEN THEATRE

Chaikin, Joseph, *The Presence of the Actor; Notes on the Open Theater, Disguises, Acting, and Repression* (New York: Atheneum, 1972) 161 pages.

——, 'Closing the Open Theatre', interview by Richard Toscan, *Theatre Quarterly*, IV, 16 (November–January 1975) 36–42.

Open Theater, The, *Three Works (Terminal, The Mutation Show, Nightwalk)*, edited by Karen Malpede (New York: Drama Book Specialists, 1974) 191 pages.

Pasolli, Robert, *A Book on the Open Theatre* (New York: Bobbs–Merrill Company, Inc., 1970) 127 pages.

3. Theatre of Social Change

THE SAN FRANCISCO MIME TROUPE

Davis, R.G., *The San Francisco Mime Troupe: The First Ten Years* (Palo Alto, California 94303: Ramparts Press, 1975) 220 pages.

San Francisco Mime Troupe, *By Popular Demand: Plays and Other Works* (San Francisco: San Francisco Mime Troupe, 1980).

Shank, Theodore, 'Political Theatre as Popular Entertainment', *The Drama Review* (T61), XVIII 1 (March 1974) 110–17.

——, 'The San Francisco Mime Troupe's Production of "False Promises"', *Theatre Quarterly* (London, TQ27), VII, 27 (Autumn 1977) 41–52.

EL TEATRO CAMPESINO

Morton, Carlos, 'Teatro Campesino', *The Drama Review* (T64) XVIII, 4 (December 1974) 71–6.

Shank, Theodore, and Adele Edling Shank, 'Chicano and Latin American Alternative Theatre', in *Popular Theater for Social Change in Latin America*, edited by Gerardo Luzuriago (Los Angeles: U.C.L.A. Latin American Center, University of California, Los Angeles, 1978) pp. 213–33.

Valdez, Luis., 'El Teatro Campesino; Interviews' by Beth Bagby, *The Drama Review* (T36), XI 4 (Summer 1967) 70–80.

——, *Actos* (San Juan Bautista, California: El Centro Campesino Cultural, 1971) 145 pages.

4. Environmental Theatre

RICHARD SCHECHNER
THE PERFORMANCE GROUP

Schechner, Richard, *Environmental Theatre* (New York: Hawthorn Books, Inc., 1973) 339 pages.

——, *Essays on Performance Theory. 1970–1976* (New York: Drama Books Specialists, 1977) 212 pages.

——, *Makbeth: After Shakespeare* (Schulenburg, Texas 78956: I.E. Clark, 1978) 53 pages.

—— and The Performance Group, *Dionysus in 69* (New York: Farrar, Straus and Giroux, 1970).

THE BREAD AND PUPPET THEATRE

Falk, Florence, 'Bread and Puppet: *Domestic Resurrection Circus*' *Performing Arts Journal*, II, 1 (Spring 1977), 19–30.

Schumann, Peter, 'With the Bread & Puppet Theatre; An Interview', by Helen Brown and Jane Seitz, *The Drama Review* (T38), XII, 2 (Winter 1968), 62–73.

—— and others, Several articles in *The Drama Review* (T47), XIV, 3 (September 1970), 35–96.

Shank, Theodore. 'The Bread and Puppet's Anti-Bicentennial: *A Monument for Ishi*', *Theatre Quarterly* (London), V, 19 (September–November 1975) 73–88. With 28 photos by the author.

Towsen, John, 'The Bread and Puppet Theatre: *The Stations of the Cross*' *The Drama Review* (T55), XVI, 3 (September 1972) 57–70.

SNAKE THEATER

Weiner, Bernard, 'Theater in Sausalito: Snake's Masks and Puppets', *Theater* (Yale School of Drama), X, 1 (Fall 1978), 84–9.

Wren, Scott Christopher, 'Snake Theater Here and Now', *New Performance* (San Francisco), I, 4 (1979).

5. New Formalism

ROBERT WILSON

Wilson, Robert, '*A Letter for Queen Victoria*' in *The Theatre of Images,* edited by Bonnie Marranca (New York: Drama Books Specialists, 1977) pp. 46–109.

——'. . . I Thought I Was Hallucinating', *The Drama Review* (T76), XXI, 4 (December 1977), 75–8.

——, '*The $ Value of Man*' in *Theater* (Yale School of Drama), IX, 2 Spring 1978), 90–109.

—— '*I Was Sitting on My Patio This Guy Appeared I Thought I Was Hallucinating*' in *Performing Arts Journal* (11/12), IV, 1 and 2 (1979) 201–18.

SUZANNE HELLMUTH AND JOCK REYNOLDS

Shank, Theodore, 'California Cool: Soon 3, Hellmuth–Reynolds, Snake Theater', *Performing Arts Journal* (12), IV, 3 (1980) 72–85.

ALAN FINNERAN
SOON 3

Finneran, Alan, 'An Interview' by Michael O'Connor, *New Performance* (San

Francisco), I, 4 (Winter 1979) 14–22.

Simmer, Bill, 'Soon 3's *Black Water Echo*', *The Drama Review* (T75), XXI, 3 (September 1977) 109–12.

Solomon, Rakesh H. '*A Wall in Venice/3 Women/Wet Shadows:* Alan Finneran's Performance Landscape', *The Drama Review* (T79), XXII, 3 (September 1978) 95–106.

MICHAEL KIRBY
THE STRUCTURALIST WORKSHOP

Carroll, Noel, 'The Mystery Plays of Michael Kirby', *The Drama Review* (T83), XXIII, 3 (September 1979) 103–12.

Kirby, Michael, 'The First and Second Wilderness', *The Drama Review* (T30), X, 2 (Winter 1965) 94–100.

—— 'Room 706', *The Drama Review* (T39), XII, 3 (Spring 1968) 141–8.

—— 'Manifesto of Structuralism', *The Drama Review* (T68), XIX, 4 (December 1975) 82–3.

—— 'Structural Analysis/Structural Theory', *The Drama Review* (T72), XX, 4 (December 1976) 51–68.

—— *Photoanalysis; A Structuralist Play* (Seoul, Korea: Duk Moon Publishing Co., 1978; available from *The Drama Review*).

—— 'Double Gothic: the Scenography of Michael Kirby', an interview by Brooks McNamara, *Theatre Design & Technology*, XV, 4 (Winter 1979) 20–3.

6. Self as Content

RICHARD FOREMAN
THE ONTOLOGICAL-HYSTERIC THEATRE

Foreman, Richard, *Plays and Manifestos*, edited by Kate Davy (New York: New York University Press, 1976) 229 pages.

——, '*Pandering to the Masses: A Misrepresentation*' in *The Theatre of Images*, edited by Bonnie Marranca (New York: Drama Book Specialists, 1977) pp. 12–36.

—— 'How I Write My (Self: Plays)', *The Drama Review* (T76), XXI, 4 (December 1977) 5–24.

—— '*Book of Splendors: Part II (Book of Levers) Action at a Distance*' in *Theater* (Yale School of Drama), IX, 2 (Spring 1978) 79–89.

SPALDING GRAY AND ELIZABETH LECOMPTE
THE WOOSTER GROUP

Gray, Spalding, 'About *Three Places in Rhode Island*', in *The Drama Review* (T81), XXIII, 1 (March 1979) 31–42.

—— and Elizabeth LeCompte, 'Play: *Rumstick Road*', in *Performing Arts Journal*, III, 2 (Fall 1978) 92–115.

LeCompte, Elizabeth, and Spalding Gray, 'The making of a Trilogy', *Performing Arts Journal*, III, 2 (Fall 1978) pp. 81–91.

SQUAT THEATRE

Squat Theatre, 'Answers: Making a Point', *The Drama Review* (T79), XXII, 3 (September 1978) 3–10.

Schechner, Richard, 'Anthropological Analysis of *Andy Warhol's Last Love*', *The*

Drama Review (T79), XXII, 3 (September 1978) 23–32.

Shank, Adele Edling, and Theodore Shank, 'Squat Theatre's *Andy Warhol's Last Love', The Drama Review* (T79), XXII, 3 (September 1978) 11–22.

Shank, Theodore, 'Squat's *Pig, Child, Fire!', The Drama Review* (T75), XXI, 3 (September 1977) 95–8.

—— 'Squat Theatre', *Performing Arts Journal* (New York), III, 2 (Fall 1978) 61–9.

Index

199